SUBARU
IMPREZA
WRX AND WRX STI
THE COMPLETE STORY

Titles in the Crowood AutoClassics series

SUBARU
IMPREZA
WRX AND WRX STI
THE COMPLETE STORY

JAMES TAYLOR

THE CROWOOD PRESS

First published in 2012 by
The Crowood Press Ltd
Ramsbury, Marlborough
Wiltshire SN8 2HR

enquiries@crowood.com

www.crowood.com

This impression 2021

British Library Cataloguing-in-Publication Data
A catalogue record for this book is available from the British Library.

ISBN 978 1 84797 422 8

Designed and typeset by Guy Croton

Printed and bound in India by Parksons Graphics

CONTENTS

INTRODUCTION

Anyone who doubts the importance of a competitions programme to sales of a car should take note of the Subaru Impreza story. Its makers needed a new small saloon, but from the beginning intended to run a rally programme with the most powerful derivatives of that small saloon. The hugely successful rally team caught the imagination of car buyers around the world, and the roadgoing derivatives of the rally cars became a cult in their own right. They also had a halo effect on sales of other, lesser Imprezas.

This is not a book about those lesser Imprezas. Worthy though they may have been, they were not the kind of cars that attract enthusiast interest. Instead, this book tells the story of the roadgoing WRX models and of their World Rally Championship siblings. It deliberately puts the focus on the cars that were available in the UK, while acknowledging the facts that there were multiple alternative derivatives available around the world and that the cars originated in Japan. UK enthusiasts have always shown an interest in the overseas models – not least because the Japanese domestic-market cars often had more power and extra features – and this book treats the non-UK models from that viewpoint.

There have been three generations of Subaru Impreza WRX, and all of them are covered in this book. All of them had 'works' rally derivatives, although the career of the third-generation cars was cut dramatically short when Subaru decided not to continue funding a rallying programme during the 2008–2009 economic recession. All of them also gave rise to myriad special editions, and there are details of all of these in this book (although it would not be a surprise to discover that a few have slipped through the net somewhere). I make no apology for the fact that these special editions are listed in tables: this is simply the most effective way of presenting the information about them.

As this book goes to press, in 2012, a fourth-generation Subaru Impreza is just around the corner. Whether it will give rise to a competition derivative in the way its predecessors did is still a question unanswered except by those at Subaru. One way or another, the future for the new model could still prove as exciting as the past was for its predecessors.

The Impreza has always been built for world markets, and as a result there have been very many minor variations to suit local requirements, and of course a large number of limited editions with specifications to suit local conditions. In trying to establish the detail of the main special editions, I have drawn on a very large number of sources, both printed and online. Sometimes, these sources have proved contradictory, so I can only hope that my interpretations of them have been the correct ones. It is also quite possible that I have missed something, somewhere!

Special thanks for assistance in putting this book together must go to Prodrive, whose PR man Ben Sayer provided a number of the magnificent images used here. My long-term colleague, photographer Nick Dimbleby, also dug out some pictures he took many years ago of the cars when they were new. In fact, it was he who gave me my first trip in an Impreza when we went on an assignment together back in 1999 and images of that very car are included in this book.

One note is worth adding for the benefit of newcomers to the Impreza scene. In the UK, enthusiasts refer affectionately to their favourite cars as 'Scooby', which seems to derive from the similarity between the pronunciation of the name 'Subaru' and that of the cartoon dog Scooby-Doo!

James Taylor
Oxfordshire, March 2012

Subaru Impreza WRX STI from 2005.

CHAPTER I

THE SUBARU STORY

Such is the image associated with the Subaru Impreza today that it is very easy to forget its origins as an affordable medium-sized family saloon for a company that was trying to make its mark on the world stage. Before the Impreza, Subaru had no real image at all, despite some promising products during the 1970s and 1980s. Good though they may have been in their own way, the Leone (sold without that name in the UK), the Rex and the Justy were solid and dependable means of transport that failed to set the world alight, and have relatively little interest for today's car enthusiasts. Even the Legacy is mainly remembered because its name has continued in use into the 21st century. But the Impreza became something else altogether.

AERO ORIGINS

Like many of today's car manufacturers, Subaru can trace its origins to the aero industry. In fact, it did not begin building cars at all until 1954. The company was originally established in May 1917, under the name of the Aircraft Research Laboratory, at Ota, in Gunma Prefecture, about 70km (45 miles) to the north of the Japanese capital Tokyo. Aircraft manufacture was an exciting and expanding new field, and this was the first aircraft company to be established in Japan. The driving force behind it was a former naval engineer called Chikuhei Nakajima, while the financial backing came from a wealthy textile manufacturer. During 1919 Nakajima took control and the company was renamed Nakajima Aircraft Company. This time, financial backing was provided covertly by the Imperial Japanese Army, which was already taking a keen interest in the company's products. The Japanese Navy also bought a quantity of Nakajima aircraft. From 1926, Nakajima began build-

ing Bristol Jupiter nine-cylinder radial engines, and by the end of the decade had drawn on the experience to design its own nine-cylinder radial aero engine. Now able to provide not only airframes but also engines, Nakajima forged an association with the Japanese armed forces that would be a cornerstone of its existence for the next 15 years. Nakajima designed and built many different types of military aircraft during the 1930s. It built such a reputation that it was co-opted during the Second World War by the Japanese Government to build the legendary Zero fighter alongside Mitsubishi, whose design it was. Nakajima eventually built more Zeros than Mitsubishi itself, as well as fighters and bombers of its own design, and by the end of the war was experimenting with jet fighter designs as well.

THE MOVE INTO ROAD VEHICLES

When Japan surrendered, in 1945, and the Allied Powers forbade further production and research, the Nakajima Aircraft Company was closed down. The company was broken up into a number of smaller divisions under the Fuji name, operating in several different sectors of the transport industry. With its Ota factory critically damaged by USAAF bombing, the company had to start again from virtually nothing. Among its first products was the simple, inexpensive Fuji Rabbit motor scooter in 1946, which supposedly used tyres left over from the company's days of building fighter planes. The Rabbit has since gone on to have its own cult following.

In 1953, five of the Fuji divisions were reunited as Fuji Heavy Industries, and not long after that the company's newly appointed Chief Executive Officer, Kenji Kita, suggested a move into car manufacture. The brand name chosen was Subaru, which in Japanese means 'unite'; the six

The Subaru 360 looks rather quaint today, but it did address the demand in Japan in the late 1950s for miniature economy cars.

stars on the Subaru logo, adopted in 1958, are said to represent the five divisions brought together as Fuji Heavy Industries, plus the new car division. Fuji vehicles are prominent in the heavy truck and bus fields and, in more recent times, FHI has once again developed substantial interests in military aircraft.

In the 1950s, the Japanese car industry was nothing like it is now. Focused entirely on the domestic market, it was heavily dependent on inspiration from more established makers in Europe. So the first Subaru, known initially as the P-1 model, bore more than a passing resemblance to the Morris Oxford of the day and used a 48bhp 1.5-litre engine derived from that of the Peugeot 202. Prototyped in 1954, it never entered full production, because the fledgling industry was simply unable to co-ordinate suppliers to the degree required for mass production. Only eleven Subaru 1500s were built with the original engine, plus a further nine with Fuji's own 55bhp 1.5-litre.

The second Subaru model was also distinctly derivative; this time from the Fiat 500. Miniature 'economy' cars were popular in Japan in the late 1950s, and the Subaru 360 was perfectly in keeping with the spirit of the times. Its engine was an air-cooled, two-stroke twin-cylinder of 356cc, designed by Subaru and mounted at the rear. It put out 16bhp, to give the little car a top speed of 95km/h (60mph).

Estate and even convertible versions followed, and the 360 was also exported, even to the USA, where it was known as the Subaru Maia, had a larger engine, and sold around 10,000 copies. However, *Consumer Reports* magazine did its reputation no good at all in 1969 when it singled out lack of power and lack of safety features as major concerns. It described the car as 'unacceptably hazardous' after it 'displayed shockingly deficient structural integrity' in a crash test conducted by the National Highway Safety Institute. Even so, more than 392,000 examples had been built by the time production ended, in 1971.

THE FIRST BOXER ENGINE

Subaru, of course, had already moved on from the 360 by the early 1970s. From 1961, the essentials of the 360 were incorporated into a small delivery truck called the Sambar and then, as the Japanese economy grew stronger and the market for larger vehicles began to open up, Subaru ventured a bigger saloon model called the 1000, which reached the market in 1966. European influence was still evident, perhaps most notably from the Lloyd Arabella, a German economy saloon introduced in 1959. The Subaru bore little visual resemblance to the Arabella, which went out of production in 1961 with Lloyd's demise, but it did share with it the unusual combination of front-wheel drive

By 1966, Subaru was ready with the 1000, a much larger saloon that featured the company's first flat-four engine.

At the end of the 1960s, the 360 gave way to the R2, which was another miniature economy car.
Exports to the USA were met with something approaching derision.

and a four-cylinder horizontally opposed 'boxer' engine. That engine configuration would go on to become a staple of all Subaru models, and from 1992 would give the Impreza one of its most appealing characteristics.

The Subaru 1000 was little known outside Japan, but from 1969 its engine was enlarged, from the original 997cc to 1088cc for the FF-1 model, which was made available as a saloon, a coupé and an estate. From mid-1970, the engine was further enlarged to 1267cc for the 1300G variant of the model. It was also in 1969 that the mechanical elements of the little 360 were re-packaged in a new small car known as the R2. Subaru by this stage was exporting to Europe and the USA, but had not yet made much of an impact. In Britain, for example, the Subaru name still meant absolutely nothing.

The 1970s would change all that. In 1971, Subaru introduced its new Leone medium-sized range. The cars depended on a 1361cc four-cylinder 'boxer' engine, and the initial two-door coupé model was soon followed by a four-door saloon and an estate car. With all-round independent suspension, front-wheel drive, and disc brakes on top models, the Leone was a realistic contender for lower-medium saloon sales in established markets outside Japan. Engine sizes and power gradually increased and it was a Leone – badged simply as a Subaru 1600 – that introduced Subaru to the UK in 1977.

FOUR-WHEEL DRIVE ARRIVES ...

The Leone in itself was in many ways a quite unremarkable design, in spite of its unusual flat-four engine configuration. Its styling was slightly awkward, as was the case with many Japanese cars of the time; it had the same long-bonnet, short-boot proportions favoured by Nissan in the early 1970s. But from 1972, it did have one distinguishing factor in its favour: a four-wheel drive option, introduced initially for the estate variant only and intended to appeal to business users. That option was another key characteristic that would help to create a distinctive identity for the Subaru brand, and would later prove fundamental to the success of the Impreza. The Leone achieved one of its key objectives, which was to help give Subaru a viable presence in the USA. One model was even awarded the Import Car of the Year title by the influential *Road & Track* magazine. At the same time, the company had not neglected its domestic market, and in 1972 it introduced a new small saloon called the Rex. This replaced the R2 model,

From 1971, the medium-saloon range was the Leone. This is the 1400 estate derivative, again with a flat-four engine. It also featured four-wheel drive.

From 1978, there was a pick-up derivative of the Leone range, which struck a chord among farmers and builders in Britain. This UK special edition was tricked out with decals, a bull-bar and a ladder bar, and rejoiced in the name of the MV Brat.

The Rex replaced the little R2 in 1972. It was still odd-looking, by world standards.

initially featuring the same 356cc two-stroke engine but later going on to a four-stroke, which was enlarged to 544cc in 1976 when Japanese regulations governing city cars (known as 'kei' cars to the Japanese) were relaxed. The Rex was also made available with four-wheel drive like its bigger brother, the Leone.

Subaru in the UK

Subaru cars were not sold in the UK until 1977, when imports began through International Motors. IM was set up by Bob Edmiston (now Lord Edmiston), the former sales director of Jensen Motors, who had used his redundancy payment to establish an import agency. The company began by acquiring the UK franchises for Subaru and Isuzu, both Japanese marques then virtually unknown in the UK.

Initial imports were of the Leone, which was available only with a 1.6-litre engine and was badged as a Subaru 1600. This was followed, successfully, by the 1800 pick-up, a four-wheel-drive derivative of the Leone Station Wagon (estate), which captured a worthwhile slice of the market for small pick-ups. Other models followed.

Subaru also has strong links with the UK through its association with Prodrive, the Banbury rally preparation specialists.

...AND TURBOCHARGING

The Leone was replaced by a second-generation model of the same name in mid-1979, and this two-model range took Subaru into the 1980s. This was the period when manufacturers were struggling to find ways of reducing fuel consumption while increasing performance. It was a seemingly impossible task that was initially approached by the widespread use of turbocharging. Subaru followed the trend and, from the end of 1983, was offering turbocharged derivatives of both the Rex and the Leone, combining the new technology with automatic transmission and four-wheel drive. Another of the building blocks of the future Impreza was now in place.

Expansion was an obvious next step for Subaru, and the mid-1980s saw the launch of two more model ranges. First came the Justy, in 1984, a small front-wheel-drive hatchback with three-cylinder engines of 1 and 1.2 litres, a CVT (continuously variable transmission) belt-driven auto-

matic gearbox, and the option of four-wheel drive. The latter was extremely unusual in this class of vehicle.

While the Justy sold well, Subaru's second new design met with only limited success. The 1985 Alcyone XT was drawn up as a two-door sports coupé, featuring quite extreme wedge-shaped styling, which was a radical departure from the rounded designs seen on other Subarus of the time. The car also featured a range of new technology, and over the years was available with options for front-wheel drive, selectable four-wheel drive, and permanent four-wheel drive.

However, its key problem was that Japanese tax regulations restricted the initial release to a 1.8-litre engine with optional turbocharger. Outside Japan, the car was generally considered to be badly underpowered. As a result, from 1987, Subaru introduced a much more powerful 2.7-litre alternative, which was classified as a luxury car on the Japanese home market because of its engine size. This ensured that domestic sales volumes would remain low. The Alcyone XT was an experiment that was not repeated; its place in the Subaru line-up was taken from 1989 by the completely new Alcyone SVX.

The original Alcyone had also somewhat muddied public perceptions of what Subaru stood for. The flat-four engines, turbocharging, and four-wheel-drive systems were popular, but it was difficult for many people to reconcile models as different as the Rex and Justy with the Alcyone XT and, although the introduction of four-wheel-drive pick-up versions of the original Leone in 1978 had done world-wide sales no harm at all, the Subaru range seemed to lack coherence. If the models had anything at all in common, it was quirkiness. Once upon a time, a company like Citroën had been able to trade on such a characteristic, but times had changed.

PIONEERING TECHNOLOGY

The Alcyone XT proved to be just a first step up the ladder: the mid-1980s also saw Subaru busily designing a second new model, which was always intended as the flagship of the range. One of its original aims was to give Subaru a viable alternative in the US market to the strong-selling Honda Accord and Toyota Camry. The plan was also to create high-performance derivatives that would take sales from such cars as the BMW 3 Series. In order to attract as many customers as possible, the new Legacy was drawn

The Justy was Subaru's entry in the small hatchback market from 1984. This is a UK-market 1.2Si model, with four-wheel drive.

The Alcyone took Subaru into the coupé market in 1985. Despite fashionably sharp styling, it was still rather oddly proportioned.

The Rise of the Japanese Car Industry

Subaru's progress in world markets in the early days was similar to that of other Japanese car manufacturers. The company's first aim had been to satisfy domestic demand, and Japanese conditions in the 1950s were very different from those in other countries. The roads were not smooth and well-made highways but rutted rural tracks where high speeds were simply out of the question. It is no surprise that the original Toyota LandCruiser emerged in this period; such a vehicle was a necessity in some areas of the country.

As high speeds did not figure in the Japanese conception of the car, suspension, road-holding and brakes were not developed to the levels expected in Europe and the USA, and early attempts to sell Japanese cars abroad mostly met with disappointment. However, massive development within Japan from the early 1960s created road conditions that were more like those in Western countries. As other Japanese industries began to enjoy export successes, so the car industry developed new products that had real appeal outside Japan.

Productivity rose during the 1960s, enabling investment in new models. The Japanese Government also intervened to

strengthen its domestic motor industry, in some cases bringing manufacturers together in a scenario not unlike that seen in Britain at about the same time as British Leyland was formed. Under the administration of Prime Minister Eisaku Sato, Nissan acquired a 20 per cent stake in Fuji Heavy Industries, and in return Nissan began to supply some automotive components to Subaru.

Exports continued to increase throughout the second half of the decade, with the result that by 1970 the Japanese had a number of models that were potentially competitive on the world stage. The real breakthrough came after the 1973–1974 Oil Crisis, when suddenly demand for large cars dried up and those makers who had viable small cars were able to make a killing. The Japanese industry, still focused on small and medium-sized cars, was able to exploit the demand and rapidly became established in Western markets. Among the beneficiaries was Subaru.

In 1980, Japanese car manufacturers collectively built seven million vehicles, thus claiming the title of the biggest car-producing country in the world.

The 1989 SVX Coupé was a much more determined attempt to appeal. With a 3.3-litre engine and flush glazing with what amounted to half-drop windows, it was certainly an eye-catcher.

The Legacy almost took Subaru into the mainstream. This is a UK-market estate version, with the four-wheel drive and flat-four engine that ensured a Subaru was always just a little different.

up as both a saloon and an estate and, in line with expectations of the Subaru marque, it came with either front-wheel drive or four-wheel drive.

With the Legacy also came a new engine. Still a four-cylinder boxer type, it had a 2-litre swept volume, a turbocharger, and an output of 217bhp. Known as the EJ series engine, it was both quieter and more powerful than the earlier EA series. And with this engine, the last of the key building blocks necessary for the creation of the Impreza was now in place.

The Legacy was something of a technological pioneer in other areas, too. Optional features included a water-cooled intercooler, four-channel ABS, a dual-range manual transmission, a computer-controlled four-speed automatic transmission, and 'hill holder' brakes, which prevented the car rolling backwards on steep slopes. It was also pos-

sible to have a height-controlled air suspension, which lowered the vehicle at speeds above 80km/h (50mph) to give greater stability, and also allowed the driver to raise the vehicle to give greater underbody clearance in rough terrain.

MOTORSPORT: EARLY DAYS WITH THE LEONE

Since 1980, Subaru's plans to give the marque an identity had also embraced a motorsport programme. It was a familiar way of raising a manufacturer's profile – as long as it enjoyed some success. There was surely little doubt about the way to go – with four-wheel drive available on most models, Subarus were ideally suited to the conditions of the World Rally Championship – but tackling such a prestigious series head on at this stage would have been foolhardy. It was deemed much more sensible to test the water with a few entries and to build experience over a period of time.

The time was certainly right. In 1979, the rallying world's governing body changed the regulations to permit four-wheel-drive cars. Although most manufacturers were initially cautious about the cost and complication, by March 1980 the German Audi brand was showing its four-wheel-drive Quattro coupé at the Geneva Show. Although the initial Audi entries with Hannu Mikkola at the wheel were officially described as being for test purposes, the car soon demonstrated the convincing superiority that later made it a legend in the World Rally Championship. Subaru's approach was a gradual and careful one, beginning with a few trial entries and then gradually building on the experience garnered from these until the company believed it was in a position to make a proper assault on the World Rally Championship. It was in many ways a sensible approach, risking very little; it was also, arguably, characteristically Japanese, in that it avoided the risk of failure and consequent humiliation until there was a very strong chance of success.

Subaru started in a small way during 1981 with a pair of Leone hatchbacks entered for the Safari Rally in East Africa by Subaru Rally Team Japan. Driver Takeshi Hirabiyashi managed 18th place overall and claimed the Group 1 award, but despite the promising start, there was a very long way to go. The strategy at this stage was to enter only a limited number of events each year, thus automatically excluding any possibility of finishing among the winners at the end of the season. The Leone went on in this way for the next few years, gradually building the experience that would be needed for an all-out assault on the WRC.

There were creditable results during this period. In the 1983 Safari, Yoshio Takaoka and Shigeo Sunahara brought their Leone home in fifth place overall with a first place in Group 2, while F. Takahashi claimed seventh overall. Most noticeable was the number of other, private entrants who were using the Subaru Leone – the word was clearly getting out. That same year, New Zealander Peter 'Possum' Bourne and co-driver Ken Fricker claimed a Group A win and 14th place overall with the RX Coupé derivative of the Leone in the Sanyo Rally of New Zealand.

In the following season, there were entries in the Monte

Carlo Rally, the Safari and the New Zealand Rally. Shekhar Mehta claimed 14th overall on the Monte, an event not especially suited to the Subarus, while Tony Fowkes managed 12th place with a class win on the Safari. In New Zealand, it was Peter Bourne again who took Group A honours and finished eighth overall, while the semi-works-entered Leone driven by Tony Teesdale finished in ninth place.

For 1985, things moved up a notch. Subaru Rally Team Japan began using the new 1.8-litre RX Turbo version of the Leone, tackling the Safari as a first outing. Carlo Vittuli and Robin Nixon brought their car home at the head of Group A and claimed 10th place overall. In New Zealand, Peter Bourne came eighth, followed by other RX Turbos in 10th and 12th places. There was more success from a privateer in the Côte d'Ivoire Rally, with an excellent sixth place, but this did not count towards the team title. The points from the other events, however, did: Subaru finished the season with 12th place in the WRC team championship.

As a result of its success in 1985, the team risked a fuller programme of events for 1986. In the Swedish Rally, Roger Ericsson came home eighth. On the Safari, the Leone 1800 RX Turbos came sixth with Mike Kirkland at the wheel, and seventh with Frank Tundo; and, despite Peter Bourne's forced retirement during the event, Subaru again took a class win. New Zealand was a less happy occasion, and the team was withdrawn after a fatal accident involving a Dunlop technician. In Argentina, an RX Turbo from Chile finished eighth, and in America, Peter Bourne took an eighth place with a private entry.

In 1987, Subaru tackled the Monte Carlo Rally again, and returned with a 12th place earned by Per Eklund and Dave Whittock. For the Safari, four of the new RX Turbo fastback coupés made their debut in the rally team, and carried off the Team Prize; Per Eklund finished fifth; Ari Vatanen tenth, and Peter Bourne eleventh. But the best result that year came from Bourne in New Zealand, with a third place for the old RX Turbo – the only podium finish that Subaru ever achieved during the Leone years. On the Côte d'Ivoire Bandama Rally in September, the Group N prize and ninth place both went to privateer Fredrik Donner, the first person ever to finish this notoriously punishing rally in a production car. In the RAC Rally in Britain, Roger Ericsson came tenth (suspension problems obliged Peter Bourne to retire). Subaru ended the season in tenth place with 11 points; it was a good placing, but they still had a long way to go to catch that year's leaders Lancia, who had finished with 140 points.

For 1988, Subaru managed their best overall WRC placing yet, ending the season in ninth place. The results that counted were sixth (Ian Duncan) and ninth (Peter Bourne) in the Safari, and a fifth place from Chilean privateers José Celsi and Elvio Olave in Argentina. Peter Bourne did not finish in New Zealand that year.

All these results were very encouraging, and Subaru top management decided it was time to change gear and commit the company to a full-scale WRC rallying programme. So in the early spring of 1988, the first steps were made in that direction, with the setting-up of Subaru Tecnica International, more commonly known as the STI division. (Over the years, the initials of Subaru Tecnica International have variously been represented as STi and STI, and the stylized logo can be read either way! For consistency, the all-capital form, STI, is used here.) Established on 2 April 1988 in Mitaka, a city within the Tokyo Prefecture, its mission was to oversee Subaru's motorsport activities, to develop and manufacture associated components for sale, and to train technicians as required. At its head was Noriyuki Koseki, who had already been at the heart of Subaru Rally Team Japan.

For 1989, STI was the named entrant in a number of WRC events that Subaru entered. This first season for the new company was unfortunately somewhat patchy, but in fairness it was to be the last season for the Leone-based cars, and work was under way behind the scenes on their replacements. On the Safari, Peter Bourne came seventh and Jim Heather-Hayes ninth. Bourne was excluded in New Zealand and had to retire his STI-entered RX Turbo in Argentina, where José Celsi and Olave also retired after an accident. Bourne's tenth place in the Australian Rally was not enough to provide Subaru with a worthwhile overall WRC ranking and the team finished in 12th place overall with just seven points.

COMING GOOD: THE LEGACY IN MOTORSPORT

The new car that STI were working on was of course the Legacy, introduced in the showrooms during 1989. That year saw a pair of turbocharged four-wheel-drive rally prototypes tested in Kenya. Meanwhile an alliance had been forged with Prodrive in England to develop and build fur-

Prodrive

Prodrive has played a major part in the motorsport success of the Subaru World Rally Championship cars and has also developed and marketed a number of special editions of the Impreza cars. The company has its headquarters in Banbury, Oxfordshire, and its core business has always been the design and construction of competition cars on behalf of manufacturers. More recently, it has also expanded by creating an automotive technology division, which provides consultancy services to manufacturers.

Prodrive was founded in 1984 by Ian Parry and David Richards, and its first major contract was with the Rothmans Porsche Rally Team. In 1986, the company also ran an MG Metro 6R4 in British and Irish rally events, and then a year later moved into touring cars with the BMW M3 in the British Touring Cars Championship. Three successful seasons followe, with Prodrive cars taking an outright win in 1988 and class wins in 1989 and 1990. In the 1990s, Prodrive ran touring-car programmes for Alfa Romeo, Honda, Ford and Volvo.

Prodrive's relationship with Subaru began in 1990, and over a period of 18 years the Prodrive-run Subaru World Rally Team (SWRT) racked up three manufacturers' titles (in 1995, 1996 and 1997), and three drivers' titles (for Colin McRae in 1995, Richard Burns in 2001, and Petter Solberg in 2003). After 2003, however, WRC success proved harder to win, and the global recession of 2008 persuaded Subaru that it was time to focus their energies elsewhere.

Prodrive also provided performance enhancements for UK-market Imprezas, with the full support of the importers, and helped prepare a number of special edition models for UK sale.

ther cars for the 1990 European rounds of the WRC. Pro-drive, based in Banbury, had worked with BMW to prepare cars for both WRC and BICC entries. With the German company planning to pull out of WRC events, in order to concentrate on the Touring Car series, Prodrive was looking for a new WRC partner. It found that partner in Subaru.

For 1990, Subaru planned a seven-event programme with the new Legacy. First came the Safari Rally, and it was clear from the start that the team meant business: no fewer than six cars were entered, with Group A entries for Markku Alen, Ian Duncan, Mike Kirkland, Peter Bourne and Jim Heather-Hayes, and a single Group N (unmodified except for safety measures) car for Patrick Njiru. Various engine problems put four of the cars out of contention. The Kenyan event was legendary for its harsh conditions, and in 1990 only ten cars out of the total of 58 entries made it to the finish – and among them was the Heather-Hayes Legacy, the only Group A car to finish, placed sixth. Just as impressive was Njiru's remarkable eighth overall, which made him the first driver ever to complete the tough Safari in a Group N car.

Results elsewhere immediately began to reflect the extra effort that the team was putting into the 1990 season. Although Markku Alen had to retire with engine trouble on the final day of the Acropolis, Ian Duncan finished eighth overall and claimed another Group N victory with the car Njiru had used in the Safari. In New Zealand, Peter Bourne took a fifth in Group A, and in Finland Markku Alen claimed a fourth. Bourne took another fourth in Australia, although both Subaru entries in San Remo retired. In the final event of the season, the RAC Rally, both Markku Alen and Derek Warwick failed to finish. But those high placings in other events enabled Subaru to finish the season in fourth place. Suddenly, the team was really on the WRC map.

That same year, Subaru of America also took the Legacy rallying, although not in WRC events. Legacy estates took first (Gene Henderson/Ralph Beckman) and second places in the 1990 Alcan Winter Rally, which ran for 10140km (6300) miles from Seattle (Washington) to the Arctic Circle and back. Although this meant relatively little on the world stage in terms of publicity, in the context of the US market it was an important achievement for Subaru.

The 1991 WRC results were strong, too. Alen's Legacy came third in Sweden, fifth in Portugal, and fourth in New Zealand. Francois Chatriot claimed sixth in Portugal and ninth in Corsica with one of the Prodrive cars. Ian Duncan was sixth on the Safari, and a Legacy claimed the

Group N prize for a second year, this time in the hands of Michael Hughes. The three-car entry for the RAC Rally saw both Markku Alen and Colin McRae crash out, but Ari Vatanen finished in fifth place. The overall WRC placing for Subaru was sixth – a little down on 1990 but still an excellent result.

Meanwhile, privateers were increasingly using the Legacy on other events. In Britain, Colin McRae had won the British Open Championship in 1991 with one, and in fact went on to do the same again in 1992. His subsequent selection as a Subaru works driver was no real surprise. His brother, Alister, came third in 1992 and claimed the Group N title, while Richard Burns won the National Rally Championship. He, too, would later join the Subaru works team.

For 1992, the Subaru works drivers were Ari Vatanen and Colin McRae, their Legacys equipped with a new gearbox that incorporated shift buttons on the steering wheel as well as a conventional floor shift lever. Similar systems would become increasingly popular, and soon began to appear on fast road cars, especially from German manufacturers. It was a good year. In Sweden, McRae claimed Subaru's best-yet WRC result with a second place, while Per Eklund came sixth in a car sponsored by Clarion. In the Safari, Eklund and Patrick Njiru drove Goup N cars, claiming class victory for a third time with individual placings of eight for Njiru and ninth for Eklund.

The Acropolis saw McRae to the fore again, finishing fourth and winning as many stages as the eventual winner, Didier Auriol in a Lancia Delta. New Zealand saw all three Subaru entries put out of action with engine troubles, but in Finland Vatanen took fourth and McRae eighth. In Australia, it was Peter Bourne who claimed sixth after Vatanen's car had been put out with a failed transmission. The season's last event was the RAC Rally, where Vatanen finished second and McRae sixth. Cumulatively, these results added up to enough points for a fourth place in the WRC for Subaru.

The Legacy's final appearances as works entries were in the 1993 season, by which time work was already well advanced on the car that would replace it. The smaller, lighter Impreza had been introduced in the showrooms during 1992, and the works rally team had seized on it as ideal for their purposes. However, Subaru President Isamu Kawai had made clear that he did not want STI to campaign the Impreza until they had made the Legacy into a winning car.

Small cars were still an important part of the Subaru repertoire, and this Vivio went on sale in the UK in 1992, a couple of years before the new medium-sized Impreza made it to European showrooms.

So the team delivered. McRae came third in Sweden, seventh in Portugal, fifth in Corsica and, finally and gloriously, first in New Zealand. In Portugal, Markku Alen came fourth with the car that Vatanen would have driven but for injury; on the Acropolis, Vatanen crashed out; and in the Safari, Subaru clearly decided not to risk failing to win Group N for a fourth time on what they hoped would be the Legacy's last outing there, and instead entered the brand-new Vivio, which replaced the Rex in March 1992. Njiru finished, but was unplaced; the other Vivios did not complete the event.

The high placings continued elsewhere. Vatanen came second in Australia, and the RAC Rally finished with Richard Burns taking seventh place and tenth place for Alister McRae. Brother Colin, meanwhile, was at the wheel of the new Impreza, which had already been seen on the 1000 Lakes Rally and was still undergoing development and testing as a rally machine. Overall, 1993 was Subaru's best season in rallying yet. They finished third in the WRC, with Colin McRae coming fifth in the Drivers' Championship that year.

CHAPTER 2

DEVELOPING THE IMPREZA WRX

It is important to restate the point that the Impreza was not designed solely as a car for the World Rally Championship. Even though its eventual adaptation as a rally contender was considered from the earliest stages of the design and development process, the Impreza's role in the Subaru range was intended to be more mundane. It was to be a medium-sized family saloon, with an estate derivative, which would enable Subaru to maintain a presence in a highly lucrative sector of the family-car market in Japan and, as far as possible, in export territories around the world. Ultimately, the Impreza was intended to replace the Leone in the Subaru range, although the older car actually continued in production for a time while the new model established itself.

What the family-car market wanted was a medium-sized car that was practical, affordable and reliable. When the Impreza was being drawn up in the later 1980s, the idea of high equipment levels or striking design was simply not on the agenda. Family buyers at the time had not been influenced by such style leaders as BMW to the extent that they were later. They wanted an ordinary car that would serve them well, and that was what Subaru designed for them. That was why the exterior design was so ordinary, and the interior always so drably functional. Subaru chose to put its development money into other areas.

The original Impreza was drawn up to feature a range of engines from 1.5 litres to 2 litres in size. There was nothing unusual or exotic about that, but the fact was that Subaru's staple road-car engine was unusual. Instead of an in-line four-cylinder, as favoured by most of the major competitors in the family-car market, it was a horizontally opposed four-cylinder, or 'boxer' four. It had been inspired by the example of the Lloyd Arabella (see Chapter 1), and Subaru continued to favour it because of its inherent bal-

ance, which reduced vibration and removed the need for complications such as balancer shafts. It would do Subaru a great injustice, though, to suggest that its design had stood still: the engine that the Japanese company had in production by the end of the 1980s was a far more modern and sophisticated powerplant, featuring all-alloy construction and electronically controlled fuel injection.

The boxer four also brought with it some key advantages that would prove of great benefit to the rally car that Subaru eventually designed on the basis of the otherwise mundane Impreza. For a start, with two pairs of cylinders lying horizontally rather than standing up straight, it was a compact engine, with all its weight low down. That would ultimately prove good for such requirements as cornering stability.

Also advantageous was the fact that the boxer's low height enabled Subaru's engineers to locate it exactly on the centre-line of the car; conventional engines, with cylinders positioned vertically above the crankshaft, were often too tall to fit under the low bonnets that designers wanted, and had to be tilted to one side or the other. This not only affected weight distribution but also, on cars with drive to the front wheels, the arrangement of driveshafts. With the engine located dead in the centre, Subaru could have equal-length and equal-weight driveshafts to the front wheels. This in turn reduced the effects of 'torque steer' under acceleration.

ALL-WHEEL DRIVE

The plan was always to build the majority of Impreza models with the all-wheel drive that had become the company's trademark. Subaru knew that it appealed to their customers, knew its practical advantages, and recognized that it helped to make their cars distinctive. It did not matter

It is important to remember that the Impreza's primary task was to replace the Leone as Subaru's medium-sized saloon. This is one of the more ordinary models: dating from October 1994, a 1992 UK-market 1.6LX saloon with two-wheel drive. It looks undistinguished, to say the least.

This 1994 1.8GL model lacks excitement, too, although it does have the benefit of drive to all four wheels. The proportions of the basic saloons always looked awkward.

that it had given Subarus the image of being farmer's cars in some areas, including the UK. In practice, relatively small numbers of Imprezas were built with drive only to the front wheels. These were entry-level models with small engines, which would have lost too much power through an all-wheel-drive system, and which were in any case not likely to be used in conditions where drive to all wheels would be necessary. Deleting drive to the rear wheels saved costs, too, and enabled the cars to be priced more attractively.

(It is worth noting that Subaru usually marketed its system with the description 'AWD', or 'all-wheel drive', even though UK press releases in the early days referred to 'four-wheel drive'. The intention may have been to distance Subaru's application of the system for everyday road use from its use on the much larger and heavier off-road vehicles – SUVs to the Americans – that used four-wheel drive.)

There was one very obvious additional benefit of engineering the Impreza for all-wheel drive. Four-wheel-drive rally cars were the latest success story, and the Subaru World Rally Team Legacy cars had demonstrated very clearly the advantages of having all wheels driven. For the eventual rally derivative of the Impreza, then, the all-wheel-drive system could only be a plus. As engineered for the Impreza, the all-wheel-drive system had a limited-slip rear differential and a viscous coupling in the centre differential. In normal conditions, the viscous coupling apportioned torque equally between front and rear wheels, but if one pair of wheels began to slip it could divert more torque to the other pair, to give maximum traction.

The flat-four engine was an essential ingredient in the Impreza formula. This is it in classic 2.0-litre turbocharged form. The air-to-air intercooler was placed horizontally above the engine at the back, where it was fed with cold air through the bonnet scoop. On the later WRC cars, however, the intercooler was located more conventionally ahead of the engine.

THE MECHANICAL ELEMENTS

The first stage of the Subaru project was to establish a target size for the car, and that was eventually translated into production dimensions of 2520mm (99.2in) wheelbase, 4350mm (171.5in) overall length, 1690mm (66.5in) width and 1415mm (55.7in) overall height. With the basic package size of the Impreza agreed, the engineers set to work on the mechanical specification; dimensions could be juggled slightly if necessary, but there could be no significant deviation from the original plan without a major re-think of the whole project.

The man who led the engineering side of the Impreza project was Takeshi Ito, who reported to the overall head of the project, Hideshige Gomi. From the beginning, it was

clear that both time and development costs could be saved by using components that were already in production for other ranges, and in practice a great deal of the Impreza's engineering specification came from the Legacy. An eventual rally car was always in the back of the mind of the project team, but it was important to get the basic engineering of the family car right first.

Notable among the elements 'borrowed' from the Legacy was the all-round independent suspension. This used MacPherson struts on the front wheels, together with L-shaped lower control arms. At the rear, there were MacPherson struts again, with trailing arms for location and parallel transverse links. The Impreza team decided that high-performance derivatives of its car should have anti-roll bars front and rear.

Flat-four engines were used in all varieties of Impreza. This is the 2.0-litre engine in a 2006 2.0R model for the UK market. To WRX enthusiasts, it looks odd without an intercooler on top.

The basic layout of the Impreza was always very simple. This 'chassis' actually belongs to a second-generation car, but is fundamentally unchanged from the original. There is strut suspension all round, the engine is pushed right into the nose of the car, and there is drive to all four wheels.

The two larger engines in the Impreza were also borrowed from the Legacy: the EJ18 1.8-litre and EJ20 2.0-litre 'boxer' types, with all-alloy construction. They were further developed for the Impreza, with two camshafts for each bank of cylinders to operate the four valves that served each cylinder. The Impreza range needed smaller-capacity units as well, of course, and new EJ15 1.5-litre and EJ16 1.6-litre derivatives were drawn up to fit the bill. These shared the all-alloy construction of the larger engines, but had the earlier, simpler architecture, with a single overhead camshaft on each cylinder bank to operate the four valves of each cylinder.

All the flat-fours had a distinctive rasping, burbling exhaust note, created by the slightly uneven firing pulses of the engine, and this would later become one of the characteristics that was best loved by enthusiasts. But it was only after the basic engineering of the car had been established that the engineers moved on to look at the potential for the high-performance car that the company needed for its rallying programme.

ENTER THE WRX

Exactly when the name 'WRX' came into being is not clear, but its meaning was fairly obvious. The letters 'WR' stood for World Rally, while the 'X' stood for 'cross-country'. The name sounded good, too. In order to become eligible for World Rally Championship events, the basic car had to be in regular production, and the Subaru engineers were sure they could deliver a performance model that would sell well to enthusiast drivers. At the time, the benchmark performance car in Japan was the third-generation Nissan Skyline GT-R, which had been introduced during 1989. This all-wheel-drive machine was certainly somewhere in the back of the mind of the engineers as they drew up the WRX derivative of the Impreza.

For the WRX, the obvious engine choice was a turbocharged version of the new four-cam 2.0-litre type. Turbocharging was by no means new to Subaru, and there were already turbocharged engines in the Legacy. None, however, had the 240bhp that the newly developed 2.0-litre turbocharged engine could muster. With this much power in a car designed to be small, light and agile, the possibilities looked very promising.

A close-ratio version of the gearbox intended for the Impreza would add its own benefits, as would a quicker steering rack, which would have power assistance as standard, just like the lesser Imprezas. The anti-roll bars were stiffened to minimize body roll. Where the ordinary Imprezas had drum rear brakes, the WRX models were fitted with discs all round, those at the rear being slightly smaller than those at the front, and the all-disc system came with a tandem servo. Although highly desirable in a high-performance car, ABS added to the manufacturing cost, so Subaru decided to make it an extra-cost option to help keep the basic showroom price of the WRX at a sensible level.

The suspension, too, was to be special. Although it shared its layout with the ordinary Imprezas, Subaru's engineers made it much harder by fitting unique springs, special bushes and stiffer anti-roll bars. The front anti-roll bar was attached by ball-jointed links, and the lower arms of the front suspension were cast from aluminium alloy. The dampers were special as well, and incorporated a linear control valve. To ensure that there was plenty of fuel available for the long stages of a rally, there was a 60-litre (13-gallon) fuel tank in place of the 50-litre (11-gallon) type fitted to the ordinary Imprezas. It was a sound move: the turbocharged Impreza could be very thirsty indeed when driven hard.

The brief given to the engineers working on the Impreza project was to deliver a viable high-performance road car. For further tuning, it would be handed over to specialists. It would be the task of Subaru Tecnica International to develop special versions with more performance, while the World Rally Championship cars themselves would be handed over to a specialist engineering company. The British company Prodrive had been working with the Subaru World Rally Team Legacy cars since 1990, and was an obvious choice to prepare and run their Impreza WRX successors.

THE BODY

The buying public was not going to expect anything startling to look at when the Impreza reached the showrooms, so the design teams working to Masashi Takahashi drew up a body shape that was almost deliberately ordinary. To Western eyes, the Impreza simply blended into the background but, paradoxically, the anonymous looks became an important part of the appeal of the high-performance models. There was an element of Q-car or Stealth Fighter about their approach: they did not look special but they did have the performance to startle drivers of many more expensive and overtly performance-oriented cars. This remained the case even when they were painted in the blue of the World Rally Team and decked out with big spoilers and a loud exhaust.

The saloon and estate bodies were drawn up to be strong so that they would meet crash regulations in the countries where the Impreza was to be sold; it was notable that the doors came with side-impact beams as standard – primarily, no doubt, to suit regulations in the USA. Yet the body was engineered to be light, too, so that even the smallest-engined derivatives could achieve respectable performance. Later, there would be a two-door derivative as well, usually known as the coupé body and initially released in a Japanese-market model called the Impreza Retna.

An interesting feature on all these bodies was that the doors had frameless windows; Subaru claimed that this was a way of reducing production complications, but it certainly also added character to a body shape that was otherwise rather dull. Durability was already a Subaru hallmark, and so production was planned around a carefully rustproofed body shell. The underside – floor pan and wheel wells – was made of galvanized steel, while all the other panels were undersealed, coated or wax-injected.

All the basics remained in place when the Subaru engineers developed the WRX cars. The saloon body shell was an obvious choice, as the estate was heavier, and some work went into lightening this. The bonnet was replaced by a specially designed derivative made of aluminium, incorporating air vents to keep under-bonnet temperatures down, and a huge air scoop right over the intercooler that was located on top of the engine at the back of the engine bay.

A body kit was added to give the car 'street appeal' through a more aggressively sporting appearance. It included side skirts, a deeper rear valance, a special grille and deep front spoiler. Two strokes of genius gave the car real distinction: at the front, the spoiler incorporated cutouts for two huge round driving lamps, which would supposedly be needed on rally stages; at the rear, the boot lid carried a large spoiler of the type used to improve downforce and therefore traction and handling on a competition car travelling at high speed. No matter that the showroom models of the WRX were unlikely ever to be driven

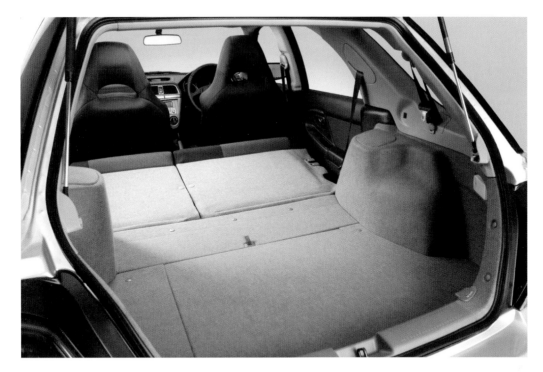

The main benefit of the five-door models was increased luggage space. The seats folded forwards, as seen on this UK-market five-door from the early 2000s.

Galvanized steel was used extensively in the Impreza body shell, and there were high-strength steel reinforcements, too. The end result was a light yet strong structure. This is the five-door body shell of a second-generation model. The side-impact beams are just visible inside the doors on the far side.

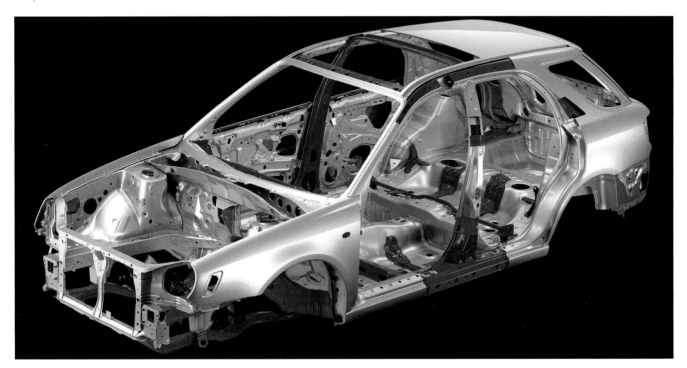

There was a five-door Sports Wagon or estate from the start. This UK-market 1.8GL model shows how the short rear deck was adapted to take an extra side window to create the estate body. It was still not an elegant or even particularly attractive car.

at speeds at which the spoiler would make a difference. Spoilers were fashionable at the time, and the spoiler on the WRX certainly looked the part. In later years, that spoiler would grow in size and become hoop-shaped, making the earlier version look positively discreet.

A WORLD CAR

Just as the Impreza was produced with a variety of different engines, so it was engineered to meet requirements in the multiple markets across the world to which Subaru intended to export the range. These fell into four distinct groups, and within those groups there were sub-divisions governed by such issues as the requirement for left-hand or right-hand steering, as well as local cosmetic preferences.

The Japanese domestic market cars (usually known as JDM types) generally shared their specifications with other Asian countries, and Asia was the first of the four major groupings. Next came the Oceania group. Strictly, Oceania is a region centred on the islands of the tropical Pacific Ocean; within it, the major right-hand-drive market for Subaru was Australia. The third group was Europe, and the major market here was the UK, the only right-hand-drive market in the group. Finally, there was North America, where the major market was the USA.

Details of the minor specification variations developed for each individual market would fill a book larger than this one, and would make for some tedious reading. Nevertheless, the different requirements of Subaru's four major sales regions did lead to the creation of some fascinating variations and special editions. Those special editions in particular have excited enthusiasts because of their uniqueness, but perhaps most interesting of all have been the JDM derivatives of the WRX models. This is because they have almost invariably been more powerful than the export models. For more detail on the multiple special-edition Imprezas, together with their outline specifications, see page 62, 112 and 148.

THE WRX GOES ON SALE

Unsurprisingly, the WRX went on sale first in the Japanese domestic market. The car was introduced at the same time as lesser Imprezas, being displayed at the Tokyo Motor Show in September 1992 and becoming available through showrooms from 1 November. It was two more years before European – and in particular, UK – versions of the WRX were made available.

As all later WRX models, including of course those for the UK, were derived from these first Japanese-specification cars, it is worth examining them in some detail. They came in two varieties: the core WRX and the stripped-out WRX Type RA. The initials 'RA' stood for 'Race Altered',

Why 'Impreza'?

When Subaru came to choose a name for their new medium-sized car, they wanted a change from Leone. The new name had to reflect a fresh image for the company. It had to be pronounceable in every language used in the countries where the new car was to be sold and, of course, it had to have no unfortunate connotations in any of those languages.

The name chosen was Impreza. Although it sounded Italian, it was in fact a made-up word with echoes of the Italian word impresa, which means (among other things) an achievement. Its sound also hinted at the English word 'impress', which the car was most certainly intended to do.

and that version of the car was specifically intended for competition use.

All WRX models were four-door saloons at this stage; estate variants would follow later. Colour options were limited to just three: Black Mica, Light Silver Metallic and Vivienne Red. Power came from the 240bhp turbocharged 2.0-litre engine, and was put down through an all-wheel-drive system. The only gearbox option was a close-ratio five-speed manual with an overdrive top, and this was allied to a low gearing in the front and rear differentials to give maximum acceleration. Where ordinary Imprezas had a 3.90:1 ratio, the WRX had 4.11:1 gearing. This reflected the priorities needed in a rally car, where rapid acceleration is ultimately of more value than a very high top speed; for road use, the overdrive top gear ensured that fuel consumption was not increased excessively. In practice, the maximum speed of a turbocharged Impreza turned out to be quite high enough to satisfy those enthusiasts who bought one.

Despite the body-kit additions, the WRX was actually 10mm (0.4in) shorter than a standard four-door Impreza. Its distinctive features were its basic black door mirrors, its twin exhausts peeping out from under the bumper (other Imprezas had only a single tailpipe), and its wheels and tyres. Standard wear were the 15-inch five-spoke alloys that were also available on the most expensive of the ordinary Imprezas, the Edition S versions of the 1.8-litre HX model. However, for the WRX these were wrapped in fatter tyres, the original equipment choice being Bridgestone Potenza RE71s in a 205/55 size.

Inside, the WRX had supportive bucket front seats with integral head restraints, and the upholstery was in black fabric with a red patterned insert. In most respects, the interior was otherwise similar to that of the HX Edition S models, although both map light and digital clock on the dashboard had been jettisoned to save weight. The WRX did have a special gear knob and a special leather-trimmed three-spoke Nardi steering wheel, and it was possible to order automatic air conditioning. (A different air-conditioning system without the automatic temperature control feature was also available as a retrospective fit through Subaru dealers.)

All the special exterior features helped to give the WRX a distinctive look on the street, but they also added weight. The standard WRX had a dry weight of 1200kg (2640lb), which was a massive increase over the 990kg (2178lb) of the base-model four-door saloon. There was no doubt that the engine could handle the extra weight but, for buyers who were intent on using their Impreza Turbos for serious competition work, there was plenty of weight to be shed. That was a key reason why Subaru introduced the WRX Type RA as a companion model for the WRX.

The RA was really a stripped-out WRX, a homologation special with all the essentials and none of the frills. Yet it was still only 30kg (65lbg) lighter than its sister car. It dispensed with the sill extensions and rear body-kit addenda. It also had strengthened suspension components, which were touted as equivalent to those used on the works rally cars (which, of course, had not been seen when the Type RA was released). Like the core WRX, it had a five-speed close-ratio gearbox and low axle gearing, but the gearbox ratios were shorter, putting the accent firmly on acceleration rather than ease of driving.

Although the passenger cabin was much the same as in the core WRX, the RA had less soundproofing, manual instead of electric windows, a driver-controlled centre differential, and an additional dash switch which sprayed water on to the intercooler to reduce temperatures and ensure maximum efficiency during hard use. ABS was simply not available on the RA; it was seen as an unnecessary complication. Similarly, there was no wide choice of colours on offer, with the RA being available only in Feather White or Vivienne Red.

While these cars kept performance enthusiasts happy, at least in Japan, the real WRC rally cars were being prepared in Britain by Prodrive. They made their debut on events in the 1993 WRC series – and the full story of that, which led on to many seasons of successful international rally competition, is contained in Chapter 4.

THE FIRST-GENERATION IMPREZA TURBO

The Impreza Turbo is best understood in the context of the whole Impreza range, a range that was designed primarily as a medium-sized family saloon and estate with a variety of engines to suit multiple markets around the world.

However, the lesser-engined Imprezas have never appealed to car enthusiasts, worthy though they may be. The cars that have attracted attention – adulation, even – are the turbocharged models with all-wheel drive that are close relations of the World Rally Championship models. These cars represent only a small proportion of the total Imprezas built.

The Impreza Turbo caught the imagination of enthusiasts in the UK from the very beginning. At the heart of its appeal was its offer of high performance at an affordable price; its obvious rivals, such as the Ford Escort Cosworth and Lancia Integrale, were 25 to 43 per cent more expensive. Later versions and limited editions of the Subaru did become more expensive, but the car's appeal was further backed up by its success in the World Rally Championship. That success was not only for Subaru but also for Britain, because WRC drivers Colin McRae and Richard Burns figured prominently in the rankings, while British company Prodrive had the contract to prepare the works rally cars. A certain exclusivity was assured by the fact that Subaru in the UK only brought in 600 examples every year, and the Impreza's excellent reliability record ensured that it remained a good buy on the second-hand market even if insurance premiums could be high for younger drivers. So for UK enthusiasts, and therefore for the majority of readers of this book, it is the story of the Impreza Turbo in Britain that matters. The story of the car's development from the Japanese end is interesting background, but this chapter and those that follow will focus on what happened in the UK. The Impreza story in other markets also

merits a look, of course, not least because it provides a context for the numbers of 'grey imports' – privately imported cars – which have reached the UK.

THE IMPREZA TURBO IN THE UK

The story of the UK versions of the Impreza Turbo really began with the announcement at the March 1993 Geneva Motor Show of Imprezas for the European market. However, these were the ordinary family models; the turbocharged 2.0-litre variants were not yet on the agenda. Cars became available through UK showrooms in May 1993, but there were no turbocharged 2.0-litres among them. The first UK models were the 1.6i GL and the 1.8i

Looking quite tame by later standards, this is a 1994-model Impreza 2000 Turbo 4WD, one of the first cars to be brought into Britain. Although the rear spoiler is relatively subdued, the characteristic rally lights in the front apron, the bonnet air vents and the big air scoop made clear that this was no ordinary Impreza.

GL, both in four-door saloon and five-door hatchback forms. Later, from January 1994, an entry-level 1.6 LX four-door saloon was made available as well.

Although there were no turbocharged cars yet, there was at least some talk about them. In the later months of 1993, Subaru UK imported a batch of six Japanese-specification Type RS cars, the development models that eventually led to the stripped-out Japanese Type RA variant. These cars were brought in for evaluation purposes and, as the turbocharged 2.0-litre engine had not yet been homologated for the UK, they were badged as 1.8i GL models! Three went straight to Prodrive in Banbury, and the other three remained with Subaru UK until they were eventually sold.

Plans were clearly afoot to introduce the Impreza Turbo to the UK, and these plans took a significant step forward at the next Geneva Motor Show, in March 1994, when the turbocharged cars were displayed in European form. Even then, there were to be examples only for the UK and for Switzerland. The Swiss preoccupation with noise legislation was one reason why these early European cars had less power than the Japanese versions. Another reason was because Europeans generally used lower-octane fuel, so the engines were detuned to cope with the 95-octane variety. Power was reduced to 208bhp at 6000rpm from the 218bhp that was the norm in the Japanese domestic market.

In the UK, the car was initially badged as an Impreza 2000 Turbo, but it was most definitely a WRX under the skin, albeit with different gearing and with ABS as standard. The colour choice was wider in the UK than in Japan, with Black Mica, Deep Green Metallic, Flame Red, Light Silver Metallic and White on offer. With its combination of performance and price (£17,499 in saloon form with an extra £500 for the estate), buyers soon discovered that the car was an absolute bargain, and it rapidly became a huge hit, taking nearly half of UK Impreza sales.

It is worth looking in detail at what *Autocar* thought of the turbocharged Impreza on its first formal acquaintance. The road testers who wrote the report for the issue dated 6 April 1994 were unimpressed by the car's 'pretty yawn-making road presence', despite the 'dinner-plate-sized fog lights and more scoops and vents than an F16'. The road test was of a saloon, but the estate received honourable mention as being 'oddly aspected'. The interior was an 'unrelenting grey cocoon of nastily textured cloth and indifferent quality plastics'. Clearly,

Bonnet air vent of the 1994-model Impreza 2000 Turbo 4WD, in close-up. The air scoop would only get bigger ... and of course this car has the striking blue paint that reminded buyers, if not the man in the street, that it was related to the World Rally Championship Imprezas.

in some respects, the Impreza failed to impress the *Autocar* road tester.

However, driving the car was a completely different matter. It would rocket from standstill to 60mph in 5.8 seconds, could reach 100mph from standstill in 18.7 seconds, and would go on to a maximum of 220.5km/h (137mph). According to *Autocar*, 'From about 3500 up to its 7000rpm red line the Impreza delivers a smoothly consistent rush of turbo thrust. It is an addictive sensation and one that will soon have you forgiving the engine for its somewhat coarse, unrefined manners.' The Impreza proved to be 'an easy car to drive quickly on challenging roads, but really keen drivers might resent the lack of involvement in the process; this Subaru is quite content to let its competent four-wheel-drive chassis take all of the credit for a tight, well-executed corner.'

In those figures and well-chosen words, *Autocar* summed up the key qualities that would still appeal to Impreza enthusiasts nearly 20 years later. They could perhaps have added that the relative anonymity of the car's looks was also an important factor in its appeal, because other drivers did not expect this ordinary-looking four-door saloon to go that fast. The bargain-basement price was another element that contributed to its appeal when the cars were new.

Yet even driving the Impreza was not without its drawbacks. *Autocar* found its ride 'unsettling' on broken surfaces and the gearchange 'slow and rubbery' and inclined to baulk, and complained of both wind noise at speed and noticeable turbo lag. Fuel consumption was none too impressive, either. Despite 'official figures' of 9.48 l/100km (24.8mpg) for the urban cycle, 5.9 l/100km (39.8mpg) at a constant 90km/h (56mph), and 7.8 l/100km (30.1mpg) at a constant 120km/h (75mph), the reality was a shocking 12.58 l/100km (18.7mpg) overall on test. Road testers do indeed drive cars hard because that is the best way of discovering their faults, but the Impreza was a car that begged to be driven that way, and enthusiastic owners soon discovered that anywhere near 9.5 l/100km (25mpg) was a cause for major celebration.

From the start of the 1993 rallying season, Subaru's WRC contenders had been Impreza Turbo models prepared by the British company Prodrive. Based at Banbury in north Oxfordshire, Prodrive had formed a close working relationship with Subaru during the days of the Legacy rally cars at the start of the 1990s, and they recognized that there was potential for a more hardcore enthusiast's edition of the Impreza in the UK. By agreement with Subaru in Japan and with the British importers, Prodrive took 25 UK-specification cars in the spring of 1994 and created the UK's first exclusive limited edition.

With no formal name, this car was known simply as the Prodrive edition of the Impreza Turbo. The Prodrive transformation cost £3950 on top of the purchase price of the basic car, and that still made it cheaper than either an Escort Cosworth or a Lancia Integrale, as *Performance Car* magazine pointed out when they tested one in June 1994.

'Prodrive has not set out to change the world by tweaking this car, but it has succeeded nonetheless in going the extra mile that Subaru opted not to go.' That was the

Performance Car verdict when they drove the demonstrator car, appropriately registered JET 2 (JET 1 was not available, as it belonged to the 1950 Rover gas turbine car that was then in the Science Museum in London). Prodrive had left the engine and gearbox well alone, preferring to concentrate on the suspension, the interior, and some cosmetics. The latter meant new air vents in the bonnet, and five-spoke alloy wheels, which had a 16-inch diameter (an inch larger than standard) and a 7-inch rim width. This allowed the car to be fitted with wider tyres than standard – Pirelli P Zero 205/50ZR 16s, which, in tandem with the suspension modifications, gave a 'rock-hard ride', according to *Performance Car*. The suspension had been lowered and uprated, and a front anti-roll bar had been added.

In many ways, though, the most important changes had been made inside. Prodrive had thrown away the standard front seats and had replaced them with Recaro sports seats, with side bolsters that provided a decent amount of support when the car was hurled into corners at speed. The Recaros' cloth upholstery was matched in the rest of the cabin, and strips of carbon-fibre effect plastic trim on the dashboard took away the remaining gloomy greyness of the factory-original specification. As a finishing touch, a sports steering wheel was also available, but the demonstrator car had the standard type, with its integral airbag.

Without any additional performance, this first Prodrive edition has not been well remembered, but it marked an important step in demonstrating how the Impreza Turbo could be improved. It also went down well with enthusiasts in Britain and brought the Prodrive name to greater prominence among buyers: no longer was the company a remote specialist firm that prepared big-budget cars for Subaru the manufacturer. Now it had a direct connection to the enthusiast on the street.

In fact, the UK would go on to become one of the Impreza's most important markets outside Japan. Interest in the turbocharged cars was immense, and the Impreza's profile was raised even higher when a British driver, Colin McRae, was chosen to drive one in the Subaru team in 1994. When the team carried off that year's World Rally Championship title, it was inevitable that Subaru UK would seek to exploit a new opportunity. In June 1995, the first UK special-edition Impreza was announced under the name of the Series McRae. It was a very astute piece of marketing, boosted without doubt by the fact that these cars had been specially prepared by Prodrive. For fuller details of the Series McRae models, see Chapter 5.

THE 'BRAND NEW' TYPE D FOR 1997

The next significant step in the UK Impreza Turbo story was taken in October 1996 at the British International Motor Show, held that year at the National Exhibition Centre in Birmingham. The face-lifted Imprezas for the 1997 model-year were announced, known within Subaru as the 'Type D' cars and marketed in some countries as the 'Brand New' Imprezas. The face-lift amounted to a new bonnet, a new mesh grille with curved lower corners and no cross-bar, sharper-looking headlights and a slightly re-profiled rear bumper. On the turbocharged cars, the bonnet vent took on a central splitter. More important perhaps, in view of earlier criticisms of the Impreza, was the use of higher-quality materials in the passenger compartment and, as standard, a new four-spoke steering wheel with integral airbag.

The Impreza Turbo 2000 was still labouring under that name, and it did not take on all the changes introduced for its Japanese Type D counterparts. Where the Japanese verison went to 16-inch wheels, the UK cars stayed with the earlier 15-inch types. The most important UK-market change, though, was the improved driveability that had resulted from a great deal of work having been done on the engine. Three key areas were affected: the compres-

sion ratio had been raised to 8.5:1 from the original 8:1, the turbocharger had been modified, and a bigger intercooler had been fitted. All these changes reduced turbocharger lag to a point at which it was all but undetectable, while at the same time improving the torque delivery, the peak of 214lb ft now arriving at 4000rpm instead of 4800rpm. Although maximum power remained at 208bhp – significantly below what was on offer in the Japanese cars – it was now achieved at 5600rpm, which was 400rpm lower down the rev range. That represented a very worthwhile improvement indeed.

Meanwhile, the Subaru World Rally Team had a superb season, and in 1996 carried off its second championship. Most impressive was its performance during the Spanish Rally in Catalunya, and once again Subaru UK decided to capitalize on this with a specially equipped limited edition. Although it retained the standard engine tune, the Catalunya edition of March 1997 must have increased showroom traffic and played its part in keeping sales healthy during the 1997 model-year.

There was a worry, though. Although the UK editions of the Impreza Turbo were hugely respected for their performance, their handling, and their value for money, enthusiasts had not been slow to discover that the versions intended for the Japanese market had much more power

In Britain, no fewer than six regional Police forces recognized the fact that the turbocharged Impreza made an excellent chase car for their Traffic Divisions. It was fast, affordable and reliable. This 1998 model was bought by the Humberside Police.

and performance. The 280bhp available on Japanese models since the introduction of the Type D cars in September 1996 sounded a lot more attractive than the 208bhp of the UK specification. Missing out on the additional enticements of a new short-throw Quickshift gearchange and improved synchromesh was more than some UK enthusiasts could bear. Unsurprisingly, a number of companies soon began to import Japanese-specification cars to the UK in this period.

There were several reasons why the UK models did not have the same engine specification as their equivalents for the Japanese domestic market. By this stage, however, another important issue had arisen. It had become clear that, because of their relative affordability, the Impreza Turbo models were appealing to young drivers in the UK. The question of insurance premiums was, therefore, significant. With 208bhp, an Impreza Turbo was already an expensive car to insure in the UK and, for some younger would-be owners, the high premiums demanded were simply unaffordable. With the 280bhp of the Japanese specification, the problem would have been compounded, and there would inevitably have been a negative effect on sales.

The Japanese cars could not be imported willy-nilly, of course. They had to have various items changed, most obviously speedometers, which read in the Japanese km/h standard instead of the UK mph. Lights, too, had to be changed before the cars were submitted for Single Vehicle Approval, without which they could not be imported legally under UK legislation. Such import procedures could prove quite expensive, and Subaru UK would not honour the Japanese warranty, but these were no barriers to the committed performance enthusiast who was also prepared to fork out for the higher insurance premiums that accompanied the more powerful cars.

The whole business put Subaru UK in a difficult position. The so-called 'grey imports' did take some sales away from the company's franchised dealers. They also emphasized the fact to the growing band of UK Impreza Turbo enthusiasts that an 'official' import was a watered-down version of the real thing. The company resolved to take action on two fronts. First, it asked the Japanese parent company to improve the performance of the cars it sent to the UK; and second, it worked with Prodrive to produce a special high-performance tune that would be officially sanctioned.

From the start of the 1998 model-year, in autumn 1997, Subaru took its first steps in bringing the specifications of Japanese and UK-market cars closer together. Out went the 15-inch wheels and in came the Japanese-style 16-inch size, with 205/50ZR16 tyres on 7J rims, as seen earlier on the Series McRae limited edition. ABS was already standard. The cabin was given a long-overdue face-lift and, like their Japanese equivalents, the Type E Turbos now had white faces for the instrument dials, a four-spoke Momo airbag steering wheel with leather-trimmed rim, and twin airbags as standard. Although there was no change in the headline power figures, the Subaru stand at the Earls Court Motor Show in October also featured a silver Prodrive-modified car as a taste of things to come. It was called the Prodrive WR Sport.

The Prodrive modifications pushed engine power up to 240bhp and torque up to 240lb ft – not as high as the Japanese-market cars but a major step in the right direction. A number of cosmetic changes also made these cars stand out from the crowd and helped to justify their higher price. Sadly, however, when Autocar magazine tested one for its issue of 9 September 1998, it discovered that the WR Sport was actually slightly slower to 60mph than a standard Impreza Turbo, and had a lower top speed as well. Arguably, however, its main appeal lay in the fact that it was something different from the standard Impreza Turbo. Enthusiasts have always been attracted by something that is different and, in its own way, exclusive.

The test car lent to Autocar was fully loaded with the options available, and the Prodrive modifications hoisted its price from the £20,006 of a standard showroom model to £30,169. However, buyers could choose from a menu of items, so the price did not have to be that high. There were four areas where Prodrive had worked its magic. The engine package cost £1968 on its own, chassis improvements came to £3231, a body kit was £2467, and interior upgrades were £2820. It was expensive, thought Autocar, but 'vitally, the modifications don't invalidate your warranty'.

The 240bhp of the engine package were achieved by means of a modified ECU, a Ramair air filter and a less restrictive exhaust. 'A blip on the throttle reveals an engine note that's louder and throatier yet more cultured than usual,' wrote Autocar. 'Your first drive will have you reaching for the window switch to hear more.' The chassis had benefited from both uprated springs and dampers and 7Jx17-inch Speedline wheels wearing Pirelli P Zero 205/45 VR17 tyres. Prodrive could set up the chassis to suit the handling characteristics that a customer wanted, but the test car had been set up for maximum stability, with the result that it under-

In Britain, it was Prodrive that delivered the hot Imprezas rather than STI. The Banbury company was of course responsible for the WRC cars as well, and its expertise spilled over on to the road cars. This was a single-exit Prodrive exhaust, which was tuned to give more of the rumble that appeals so much to Impreza owners.

Prodrive branding was important, too: it demonstrated to other owners that a particular Impreza was not a run-of-the-mill car but a specially tuned and prepared example. Here, the Prodrive name appears on a wheel centre cap; the wheel is finished in gold, of course.

Some colours suited the car's shape better than others. The red on this 1999 model works well, and there is no need for gold wheels. This was the classic first-generation Impreza Turbo as Britain knew it – still relatively discreet but packing a huge punch.

steered more than a standard Impreza. Brakes, too, had special pads that were supposed to reduce fade and shorten stopping distances, but *Autocar* found their performance 'slightly inferior to that of the standard car'.

As for the interior, the WR Sport package brought Recaro sports front seats and three extra gauges mounted in a pod above the central air vents. The body kit – least important of all unless a buyer wanted the car to advertise its additional performance – consisted of new side skirts and door mirrors painted in the body colour, plus a taller rear 'wing' spoiler.

The 1997 rallying season had meanwhile ended with yet another overall win for the Subaru World Rallying Team, the third in a row. It was both inevitable and entirely appropriate that this success should be marked by another limited-edition model. Beginning in April 1998, Subaru UK brought in 333 examples of a model it called the Terzo. Finished appropriately in a micatallic blue paint similar to that used on the WRC cars, and wearing gold-painted wheels just as they did, the Terzo certainly looked the part.

But – and it was a big 'but' – the Terzo was nothing more than the result of a cosmetic exercise. With the engine still in standard tune, with 208bhp, it offered enthusiasts a visual treat, but could not compare with the car with which Subaru was commemorating its third WRC win in Japan. Announced in March 1998, just a month before the Terzo, the 22B-STI limited edition really did offer something different. It had a new and bigger 2.2-litre engine with 276bhp and 268lb ft of torque at a temptingly low 3200rpm. This engine had been seen in the Subaru Legacy, but not in this state of tune, and it had never before appeared in an Impreza derivative. The 22B had a quicker steering rack, uprated suspension, and wider tracks under the flared wings associated with the WRC cars. Better yet, it was based on the two-door body shell, which was not available in any form in the UK.

Unsurprisingly, as many as 50 examples of the 22B had already reached Britain as grey imports before Subaru UK got around to making a UK-specification model available. That did not happen until 1999, when the company secured 16 examples of the 25 cars made for export. The first example had been shown at the NEC International Motor Show in October 1998, and all of them passed through the Prodrive workshops for modifications that allowed them to meet the UK's Single Vehicle Approval requirements. These were, without a doubt, stunning

machines, with a 0–60mph figure of 4.3 seconds, and they are still viewed with some awe by Impreza enthusiasts in the UK today. For more details on the 22B, and its appeal, see Chapter 5.

THE TYPE F CARS FOR 1999

In the mean time, the 'standard' Impreza Turbos had all been upgraded for the 1999 model-year that began in autumn 1998. These were Type F models, characterized visually by a front-end face-lift with a new honeycomb grille, bumper and air dam, plus new multi-reflector headlights. There was also a taller boot-lid spoiler. Interior changes were limited to new upholstery on the seats and door panels, height-adjustable front seats, and a slightly different Momo steering wheel. All-round ventilated disc brakes with four-piston calipers at the front were perhaps of more interest to hardcore enthusiasts, as were the inverted damper struts first seen on the 22B. New colours must have helped sales, and the alarm and immobilizer now fitted as standard doubtless eased the pain of high insurance premiums.

Under the bonnet, the Type F models had the Phase II version of the EJ20 flat-four engine, which had made its bow a couple of months earlier in the bigger Forester and Legacy models from the Subaru stable. On manual-gearbox versions of the Impreza Turbo, like those sold in Britain, this new engine was known as an EJ207 type, and it boasted modified inlet ports, thinner piston rings to reduce friction, and a thinner water jacket as well. Better low-speed and mid-range torque were among the benefits, but the headline figure of 218bhp showed that Subaru in Japan were slowly edging towards the parity of power between Japanese and UK models that they hoped would put an end to grey imports in the UK.

There was, of course, a limited edition during 1999 to give a fillip to showroom sales. The RB5 was named after driver Richard Burns, who had just returned to the Subaru World Rally Team; 5 was the number of the car that he regularly drove. Standard cars had the regular 215bhp engine, but most were delivered with the extra-cost Prodrive Performance Pack, which boosted power to 240PS (237bhp) and torque to 350Nm (258lb ft) and made the cars much more driveable thanks to better mid-range response. With sharper handling and attrac-

The tall rear spoiler made a lot of difference to the car's appearance. Here it is on a 2000-model UK-market press car. By this stage, silver was becoming extremely popular for cars of all kinds: the conventional wisdom was that it was a 'non-colour', which did not polarise opinions and would therefore not harm a car's resale chances.

tive cosmetic alterations, the RB5 easily sold all 444 examples, which made it by far the largest UK special edition yet.

The October 1999 London Motor Show, held as usual at Earls Court, introduced the Type G models to the UK, although as usual only enthusiasts would have known (or cared) that this was the Subaru designation. According to that year's show catalogue, the highlights were not significant: 'The Impreza Turbo receives new-look alloy wheels, colour-keyed door mirrors and door handles and silver-finish centre console.' The body-colour handles and mirrors had been available in Japan for some time, and the UK had lagged behind here; the 16-inch six-spoke RAYS forged alloys were indeed new. The 'silver' finish for the centre console is more commonly described as a 'graphite' finish and had in fact been seen before on the RB5 limited edition earlier in the year. On the cosmetic side, there were also new colours for the turbocharged cars; the stand-out was probably Red Mica.

These were to be the last of the first-generation Imprezas. A new model was already on the stocks in Japan, destined to make its debut for the UK market at the Birmingham NEC Motor Show in October 2000.

UK Registrations

Many cars owned by enthusiasts in the UK were given so-called 'private' registrations with combinations of letters and numbers that had special meaning either for the owner or because of the car's type. (For example, one special-edition 22B model carried the number 228 EGO.) However, the majority of cars had a number-plate as allocated by the registration authorities, and from these plates it is possible to tell at a glance the period in which the car was registered. These periods are an approximate match for the Subaru model-year.

Prefix letter	Registration period	Model-year
L	August 1993–July 1994	1994
M	August 1994–July 1995	1995
N	August 1995–July 1996	1996
P	August 1996–July 1997	1997
R	August 1997–July 1998	1998
S	August 1998–February 1999	1999
T	March 1999–August 1999	1999
V	Sept 1999–February 2000	2000
W	March 2000-August 2000	2000

THE IMPREZA TURBO IN JAPAN

The link with the cars used in the World Rally Championship was much clearer from the beginning on Japanese-market Imprezas. Announced in October 1992, the turbocharged 2.0-litre cars were always badged as WRX types. Straight out of the box, they offered 240bhp at 6000rpm and 224lb ft of torque, figures that were astonishing for a 2.0-litre four-door car at the time. The BMW M3, launched that same autumn, needed 3 litres and 7000rpm to deliver its 286PS, was vastly more expensive and at this stage came only as a two-door coupé.

The Japanese Type A models, which came as mainstream WRX and competition-oriented Type RA models (see Chapter 2), were the 1993-season cars for the Japanese domestic market. The 1994 models were introduced at the 1993 Tokyo Auto Salon and naturally became Type B cars. This time, the existing two-model WRX range was joined by no fewer than three new models. The saloon was made available with a four-speed automatic gearbox as an alternative to the close-ratio five-speed manual, and in this guise came with a lower engine output of 220bhp at 6000rpm and 206lb ft at 3500rpm. It was additionally equipped with the Variable Torque Distribution system already seen on Subaru's Alcyone SVX sports coupé. Normally distributing 55 per cent of the available torque to the rear wheels and the other 45 per cent to the front pair, this system depended on wheel-spin sensors to divert torque to the wheels with traction and thereby improve grip and handling.

The other two models were both based on the Sports Wagon or estate model of the Impreza, and both had the same 220bhp version of the 2.0-litre engine. They came as a Sports Wagon WRX or cheaper Sports Wagon WRX-SA. Both had a roof spoiler, bucket seats and automatic air conditioning, although both the latter and the roof rails could be deleted to save money on a special-order derivative of the WRX-SA.

If this lower-power version of the engine and automatic option suggested the WRX was going soft already, new models announced in January 1994 made clear that the reverse was the case. These were the first ones to carry the STI name that would later become such a major feature of Subaru marketing. Still classified as Type B models, they consisted of a WRX-STI saloon and WRX-STI Sports Wagon, both available exclusively with manual gearboxes and both finished by hand at the Subaru Tecnica Interna-

tional plant in the Tokyo suburb of Mitaka. Clearly, limited production was the aim, as the Mitaka plant was simply not geared up for volume assembly, and in fact the original plan was to sell only 100 examples a month and to end production in September. That would have resulted in a maximum production of 900 cars.

Both saloon and estate models had the same blueprinted engine that delivered 250bhp at 6500rpm and 227lb ft at 3500rpm. Modifications from the standard WRX tune included a Mitsubishi TD05H turbocharger, forged pistons, polished inlet ports, the STI lightweight hydraulic valve lash adjuster (known as HLA), a remapped ECU and a large-diameter exhaust made by the legendary Japanese aftermarket tuner Fujitsubo. The intercooler had a water spray with STI nozzle and its ducting had been improved. An aluminium strut brace between the front suspension towers tautened the handling, and there were dark silver 15-inch alloy wheels. Options included 16-inch STI Electra R two-piece alloys and a limited-slip rear differential.

These first STI cars were distinguished externally by STI badges on the front air dam and boot lid, a cherry pink grille badge with an 'S' instead of the usual six-star logo, and a large rear spoiler. The same three colours available on the standard WRX were offered, and the interiors were in black for the saloon or grey for the estate, with

The Tommy Kaira M20b

When leading independent tuner Tommy Kaira began to modify Impreza WRX models for the Japanese market in 1993, it was an acknowledgement that the cars had 'arrived' with hardcore street performance enthusiasts.

Based in Kyoto, Tommy Kaira named their car the M20b and based it on manual-gearbox saloon versions of the WRX. Engine modifications increased output to 260bhp at 6500rpm and 242lb ft at 5300rpm. Gearing and suspension changes accompanied a special front air dam and twin-blade rear spoiler, and interior changes were also made to suit the car's aggressively sporting nature.

The company continued to modify Imprezas for the Japanese market for a number of years.

fake suede trim for the front seats and door panels, and the STI logo stitched into the seat backs. The Nardi steering wheel had a fake carbon-fibre insert, plus red stitching that was also used on the gear knob.

With the introduction of the Type C Imprezas in September 1994, the WRX-SA Sports Wagon disappeared, and the automatic versions of the saloon were also withdrawn. Subaru was already getting a clearer understanding of the market for its high-performance model, and in reflection of that the WRX and WRX-RA engines went up to 260bhp at 6500rpm and 227lb ft at 5000rpm, thanks to an increase in turbocharger boost pressure.

The STI experiment had been a great success, and so the Mitaka plant began in November to turn out another small-production car called the WRX Type RA STI. This time, the engine modifications delivered a massive 275bhp at 6500rpm and a very useable 235lb ft at 4000rpm. Work had been done on the cylinder heads, and this high-power engine also had forged pistons and a special water-spray nozzle for the intercooler. There was also a new control system for the transmission, known as the Driver Controlled Centre Differential. This allowed the driver to adjust the division of torque between front and rear wheels in five increments to suit different surfaces. In practice, it was of almost no use on the road, but it did have potential value on the loose surfaces that drivers might encounter in rallies. A new Quickshift gearchange was another welcome, rally-style, improvement, and a strut brace tightened the handling.

The WRX Type RA STI had its own cosmetic additions, too. There were WRC-style fog-light covers at the front, a tall rear spoiler, and a roof vent. The 6.5Jx16 wheels had a gold finish and came with Bridgestone Potenza 205/50 tyres, and there were Type RA badges on the wings and tail, plus a pink STI grille badge. However, it was already clear that demand for the STI cars exceeded the STI plant's ability to build them, and so these were the last STI models to be built at Mitaka. When the next iteration of the STI models arrived, in August 1995, they were built on the main Impreza assembly lines at Yajima. They were known collectively as the WRX STI Version II models. STI still had a direct input, of course, not least with hand-built engines for the WRX Type RA STI Version II, which was built only to order. Otherwise, these Version II cars came as a Pure Sports Sedan or Pure Sports Wagon, with strictly limited-edition variants called the 555 Pure Sports Sedan and the 555 Pure Sports Wagon.

The Gravel Express

The 1996 'Gravel Express' was an interesting confection, which combined the turbocharged engine with the Sports Wagon body, a raised suspension and some 'tough' four-wheel-drive design cues. The two-tone paint was one of them, recalling 4x4 SUV models from the likes of Mitsubishi and Isuzu.

The Japanese domestic market was offered a rather interesting special model for the 1996 model-year – the Gravel EX, which typified the country's taste for creating niche versions. The 'EX' was short for 'Express', and enthusiasts tend to refer to the model in full, as the 'Gravel Express'.

The car was announced a few days before the Tokyo Show in autumn 1995 in order to give Subaru an additional bite at the publicity cherry. In essence, it was an Impreza Sport Wagon that had been kitted out for rough-terrain use and fitted with the 220bhp turbocharged 2-litre engine. The general concept followed that of the Outback model, already available in North America, where it had more mundane power plants.

The Gravel Express was distinguished by roof bars and two-tone paintwork, the lower panels being in silver. It had a bull bar at the front and an external spare wheel in the fashion of off-road vehicles, plus increased ground clearance. The extra height was masked by side runners under the body sills.

The Gravel Express could be ordered with an extra-cost Touring Pack. This added front fog lights, 15-inch five-spoke wheels with 205/60x15 tyres, and a Kenwood ICE system. Multi-spoke BBS alloy wheels were also an option.

More limited-edition models followed in early 1996, as witness to the effectiveness of this form of marketing in Japan. These were the WRX V-LImIted and WRX Type RA STI Version II V-Limited, both of which are described in more detail in Chapter 5. These were the last of the Type C Imprezas; from the autumn, the Type D would take over. The basic changes introduced with the Type D cars have already been described in the section on UK models. Most important in terms of the Impreza's evolution was that the Japanese-market Type D WRX saloons now developed 280bhp, which was the maximum permitted under the Japanese voluntary agreement with the international motor manufacturing community. This new maximum was achieved at 6500rpm, and maximum torque of 242lb ft was generated at 4000rpm. Sports Wagon engines were detuned, with 240bhp at 6000rpm and 224lb ft at 4000rpm, but shared the new Mitsubishi TD04L turbocharger and lower compression ratio of 8:1. The saloons came as WRX and WRX Type RA variants, and there was a WRX Sports Wagon with automatic gearbox, which had a turbocharger with different blades.

Even the STI saloons and Sports Wagons – now Version III types – had the same 280bhp, although they had a different turbocharger, made by IHI. They also acquired four-piston front brake calipers, and ABS became standard on all WRX variants except the WRX Type RA and WRX Type RA STI Version III. There were gearing changes for the WRX models, too.

However, January 1997 brought something really new to the WRX range. Back in December 1994, a two-door 'coupé' derivative of the Impreza body had been introduced on a new model that was called the Impreza Retna in Japan. This two-door shell was to be used for the 1997 World Rally Cars, and to coincide with their launch Subaru announced a two-door WRX Type R STI Coupé. It was built to order only, featured the Type RA's close-ratio gearbox and Driver-Controlled Centre Differential, but otherwise had essentially the same mechanical specification as the contemporary WRX STI Version III. Launched at the same time was a special-edition saloon inspired by the Subaru team's success in the 1996 WRC, called the WRX STI Version III V-Limited.

Cosmetic changes apart, the range continued with the Type E variants, introduced in September 1997. ABS was standardized on all variants except the WRX Type RA, WRX STI Type R and WRX STI Type RA, and the new WRX STI Version IV cars could be had in saloon, coupé or

It was even possible to combine the best of both worlds. This is the engine bay of an imported STI model on which Prodrive have been invited to perform their magic. The logos of both companies must have been a source of some pride for the original owner.

The rev counter dominates the instrument panel and the speedometer is very much a subordinate instrument, being slightly smaller and off to the right.

The Impreza's interior was never up to much, but STI enhancements certainly helped. Red stitching on steering wheel and gear lever provide welcome relief from the otherwise drab greyness. The car has also been fitted with an aftermarket boost gauge.

White instrument dials were featured from the 1998 model-year. This is a Japanese-market STI import, with blue seat facings. The mobile-phone bracket was not standard equipment.

Although the STI-developed versions of the first-generation cars were big news in Japan, they were available in the UK only as personal imports. Ownership of an imported STI Impreza brought considerable street cred, and the cars regularly featured in performance-oriented magazines of the time. The two-door or coupé body was very attractive; this Japanese-market STI coupé dates from 1998. Note the pink 'S' grille badge and the STI logos on the light covers.

Wheels mattered: the World Rally Team cars had gold-coloured wheels, and the gold wheels on this imported STI coupé were a deliberate link to the sharp end of the Impreza business.

Sports Wagon guise. As was to be expected, the 1997 WRC victory was an essential element in the promotion of new V-Limited variants of the WRX Type RA STI Version IV saloon, WRX Type R STI Version IV V-Limited saloon, and WRX Type R STI Version IV V-Limited coupé introduced in January 1998. For more detail on those models, see Chapter 5.

The really big news was the 22B-STi model that was announced in March 1998, which combined the coupé body shell with a highly tuned and turbocharged version of the EJ22 2.2-litre engine used in US-market Legacy models. This legendary Impreza is described in more detail in Chapter 5, and of course a number of examples reached the UK as special imports even before Subaru UK managed to secure a quantity for official sale. In its native Japan, though, the 22B demonstrated the extent of interest in the turbocharged Impreza when all 400 examples of the limited edition sold out within 30 minutes, 24 hours, or 48 hours of going on sale, depending on who tells the story.

The Type F models in September 1998 brought the front-end face-lift and Phase II engine (see page 34, UK models), but as usual there were some special features on the Japanese cars. The WRX, WRX Type RA and WRX STI cars all had improved gearbox synchromesh to give smoother gear changes, and the engine-gearbox unit was made stiffer by doubling the number of bolts holding the two components together, from four to eight. The WRX Sports Wagon engine, still with a 9:1 compression rather than the 8:1 of the other models, still had the lower 240bhp power output, although torque went up slightly, to 227lb ft.

GC Models, 1992–2000

Engine
Subaru EJ20 horizontally opposed four-cylinder. Aluminium block and heads; turbocharger with air-cooled intercooler; various different types of turbocharger were used for different variants.

Capacity	1994cc
Bore and stroke	92 x 75mm
Compression ratio	8.0:1, 8.5:1 or 9.0:1, depending on variant
Fuel system	Multi-point injection
Valve gear	Four overhead camshafts (two on each cylinder bank); four valves per cylinder

Japanese-spec engines in manual-gearbox saloons:
240PS at 6000rpm with 224lb ft at 4000rpm
(1993–1994 models)
260PS at 6500rpm with 227lb ft at 5000rpm
(1995–1996 models)
280PS at 6500rpm with 242lb ft at 4000rpm
(1997–2000 models)

Japanese-spec engines in automatic-gearbox saloons and all Sports Wagons:
220PS at 6000rpm with 206lb ft at 3500rpm
(1993–1996 models)
240PS at 6000rpm with 224lb ft at 4000rpm
(1997–2000 models)

UK-spec engines:
211PS at 6000rpm and 201lb ft at 4800rpm
(1994–1996 models)
211PS at 5600rpm and 214lb ft at 4000rpm
(1997–2000 models)

STI-spec engines:
250PS at 6500rpm and 227lb ft at 3500rpm
(1994 models)
275PS at 6500rpm and 235lb ft at 4000rpm
(1995–1997 models)
280PS at 6500rpm and 260lb ft at 4000rpm
(1998 models)

[Note that the 1998 22B-STI models had a 2.2-litre EJ22 engine; see Chapter 5.]

Transmission
Permanent four-wheel drive with viscous-coupled centre differential; VTD standard with automatic gearbox; DCCD on WRX STI models from 1995 model-year.

Gearbox
Five-speed manual, with overdrive fourth and fifth gears; RA and WRX STI models with close-ratio five-speed gearboxes and overdrive on fifth gear only.

Final drive gearing
4.11:1

Steering
Power-assisted rack-and-pinion.

Suspension
Front: MacPherson struts with coil springs, transverse link, some models with anti-roll bar.
Rear: MacPherson struts with coil springs, trailing arms, some models with anti-roll bar.

Brakes
ABS available and standard on some models.
Ventilated front discs with twin-piston calipers; solid rear discs with sliding calipers.

Weights and measures

Wheelbase	2520mm (99.25in)
Front track	1460mm (57.5in)
Rear track	1455mm (57.25in)
Length	4340mm (171in)
Width	1690mm (66.5in)
Height	1400mm (55in)
Wheels	15in alloy, later 16in
Tyres	Various sizes (see text)
Unladen weight	1235kg (2723lb)

The Sports Wagon or estate body may not have been the most attractive, but the blue paint and gold wheels set it off rather well. This is a Japanese-market STI derivative.

Branding mattered, too. It was a simple matter for Subaru's STI division to have the lenses of the driving lamps on some of its cars adorned with its own logo, but it added distinction and uniqueness to the cars. This was niche marketing at its most effective.

There were new colours and equipment changes for these 1999 model-year cars, too. The WRX models could be fitted with an electric sunroof, but this was not available on the Type RA variants because of their rally-style roof vent. However, the Type RA could now have ABS, twin airbags, and automatic air conditioning, and its intercooler water spray was no longer fitted.

Then, of course, there were the latest STI models, this year sold as Version V types and again available in four variants: WRX STI Version V saloon, WRX STI Type RA Version V saloon, WRX STI Version V Sports Wagon and WRX STI Version V Type R coupé. There were new fog-light covers to suit the face-lifted front end, and the saloons and coupé took on a larger rear spoiler. The 1999-model cars had reinforced transmission casings, with a smaller and lighter centre LSD. Most had the Suretrac rear LSD, although the Type RA had a mechanical LSD. All cars had a new ABS braking system with separate rear wheel sensors, while the Type RA again went its own way with stiffer dampers and the quick 13:1 steering ratio seen on the 22B.

A couple of months later, November brought the three models of the 1999-model WRX Limited series, all of them painted in Sonic Blue Mica and sporting gold alloy wheels. These were the WRX STI Version V Limited saloon, the WRX STI Version V Limited coupé, and the WRX Type RA Version V Limited saloon. (As limited editions, these are outlined in more detail in Chapter 5.)

The last versions of the first-generation Impreza WRX were the Type G models, introduced in September 1999.

Key changes were a deeper front lip spoiler, new 16-inch six-spoke alloy wheels and new paint colours, while the core WRX gained the same body-colour sill skirts as the STI cars. ABS, where fitted, was supplemented by Brake Assist, and a starter inhibitor was fitted as a safety measure, meaning that the clutch had to be dipped before the engine would start.

The Type RA cars could be ordered with bullet-shaped door mirrors. As for the Version VI variants of the STI cars, their mechanical specification was unchanged from the previous year but the coupé and saloon models both gained a more dramatic rear wing spoiler. All except for the Sports Wagon retained the previous year's five-spoke alloy wheelsl; the Sports Wagon moved to gold six-spokes. Interiors were unchanged, but an imitation carbon-fibre trim kit became available as an accessory. Black paint also disappeared from the options list.

Finally, November 1999 brought the regular four Limited models, all painted in Sonic Blue Mica and wearing gold six-spoke RAYS forged alloy wheels. Further details of the WRX Type A Limited saloon, WRX STI Type RA Version VI Limited saloon, WRX Type RA Version VI Limited coupé and WRX STI Version VI Limited Sports Wagon are given in Chapter 5.

THE IMPREZA TURBO IN AUSTRALIA

Australia was the other major right-hand-drive market for the Impreza Turbo, so its cars have more appeal to British enthusiasts as potential imports than those from left-hand-drive territories. Broadly speaking, the evolution of the Australian WRX models followed that of the Japanese cars, although Australia was treated as an export territory and therefore received export-specification models rather than the full-house Japanese domestic-market versions.

The first WRX models were exported Down Under in March 1994. These had the same 208bhp at 6000rpm as UK-specification cars, with 201lb ft of torque at 4800rpm.

Springs were rather softer than on Japanese cars, and ABS was a standard fitment. Engine power went to 218bhp in August 1998, at the same time as it did for other export markets, including the UK.

The first limited edition was the WRX Rallye in March 1996, which was a strictly cosmetic exercise and offered nothing tangible that was not available on the standard Australian WRX. Cosmetics mattered in the Australian market, and at the end of the 1996 season enthusiasts were given a model called the RX, which looked like a WRX but actually had the naturally aspirated derivative of the 2-litre engine. This gave rise to its own limited editions.

For 1997, automatic-gearbox models were added to the Australian line-up. An automatic WRX saloon was made available from the start of the season, while an automatic WRX five-door became available alongside the five-speed car later on. The 1997 cars all gained a little extra power from turbocharger and intercooler modifications, delivering 211bhp at 5600rpm and 214lb ft at 4000rpm.

Australia's regular limited editions were the WRX Club Spec models (for more details, see Chapter 5). The first, in 1997, sold out in eight days; realizing they were working on the right lines, the Australian importers arranged a WRX Club Spec Evo 2 model for May 1998. There was a WRX Club Spec Evo 3 edition in June 1999, and the final one was a WRX Club Spec Evo 4 in March 2000. There were a number of very attractive models among these limited editions.

During 1998, Australia took five examples of the 22B special edition from the export allocation. However, it was 1999 that was a particularly good year for Australian sales of the WRX models. Imports of the STI models began at the start of the year, and the 280bhp WRX STI Version VI saloon went on sale as a limited edition in August 1999. Meanwhile, a WRX Classic limited edition in February proved such a big hit that it was duplicated in December under the different name of WRX Special Edition. More details of all these limited-edition models are given in Chapter 5.

CHAPTER 4

THE RALLYING STORY, 1993–2000

Rallying is a tried-and-tested means for a motor manufacturer of improving the breed – and increasing sales – and Subaru's determination to achieve success in the World Rally Championship was always fundamental to the way the Impreza evolved. It was also fundamental to its public perception: loud, highly tuned and bespoilered Imprezas have given a certain street credibility to their owners wherever the car has been sold, and that street credibility has had an unshakeable foundation in the Impreza's rally success. It won the Manufacturers' Championship prize in the WRC three times in a row (in 1995, 1996 and 1997), and its drivers have won the Drivers' Championship three times (in 1995, 2001 and 2003). That is a formidable record for any car.

The rallying history of the first-generation Impreza can be divided into two distinct periods. The first period lasted from 1993 to 1996, when the cars entered WRC events in the Group A category. Between 1997 and 2001, further evolved versions of the first-generation (or GC) models entered the new World Rally Car classification.

1993–1996

The FIA established the Group A category of the World Rally Championship in 1987 in response to a series of major accidents involving the ultra-high performance Group B cars, most notably the death of Henri Toivonen and his co-driver in the 1986 Tour de Corse. Group B cars had virtually no restrictions, and did not even have to be based on ordinary production models. The Group A cars, by contrast, had to be based on production models, had their maximum power limited, and had to meet a minimum weight requirement.

The World Rally Championship

The World Rally Championship was established in 1973 out of a number of existing international rallies. It is administered by the FIA (Fédération Internationale de l'Automobile, the governing body of international motorsport) and consists of a number of three-day events, typically around 15, spread throughout the calendar year. The character of these events differs, some being run on tarmac or gravel while others are run on snow and ice. Each rally has between 15 and 25 special stages, which are run against the clock on closed roads.

Points are awarded for places in each event, and the maximum number of points determines the overall championship winner. There are championships for both drivers and manufacturers within the WRC, and these are run separately. A complication is that manufacturers are allowed to nominate only two drivers from their team to score points for the team as well as scoring for themselves as individuals.

The publicity and credibility engendered by a WRC win have encouraged major manufacturers to spend enormous sums of money on creating winning cars and engaging the best drivers. For the drivers, WRC success is a ticket to high earnings and a regular place in one of the top teams.

So for Subaru, entry into the World Rally Championship automatically demanded the preparation of a car to Group A standards. The Prodrive-developed Legacy models with which they entered the 1990s were Group A cars, and the Imprezas would also be Group A cars until the new World Rally Car classification was introduced for the 1997 rallying season.

Right from the start of the 1993 season, the Subaru team cars were all painted in the new team colour of blue, with yellow '555' lettering. This reflected their new major sponsor, State Express 555 cigarettes, a brand owned by British American Tobacco that was popular in the Asia Pacific region. These cars are often referred to as the 'Impreza 555' cars, and all had left-hand drive.

Most of the Group A cars wore UK registration numbers containing the numbers 555. However, the numbers were almost certainly swapped among cars, particularly when a 'spare' car had to stand in after a car had been put out of action in an accident. The result is that these registration numbers are not a reliable way of distinguishing one car from another. As Graham Robson has explained it, in *Rally Giants – Subaru Impreza*, behind the identity of N1 WRC, the number on every car that Colin McRae drove in the 1996 WRC season, lay a car that had been 'crashed several times, rolled badly in Argentina, and was totally wrecked in Finland. So much for registration numbers...'. Registration numbers are a (slightly) more reliable guide to the identity of the later cars, because there was a crackdown on swapping cars' identities after the introduction of the new WRC rules for 1997.

Two of the first-generation rally cars had numbers that did not conform to this pattern. The first was registered as L408 FUD. It was an early publicity car that was almost certainly also a spare car for the rally team. The second was the car registered as N1 WRC, which was one of the new team cars for the 1996 season.

Rally cars take a terrific pounding, and it is standard practice in world-class rallying for cars to be completely rebuilt between events. Apart from replacement of the more obvious consumable items and any others that have become damaged or worn, the body shells are completely rebuilt to ensure that the structure will be able to withstand the strain of the next event without failure. In 1993, each body shell rebuild took 160 hours.

All the team Imprezas were prepared by Prodrive in the UK, and from the beginning they benefited from the company's experience with the Group A Legacy rally cars.

Engine power was quoted as 300bhp, the maximum permitted under the Group A rules, with 339lb ft of torque at 5000rpm. In practice, the power may well have been more; the rules insisted on restrictors to limit maximum power but were otherwise not very strictly enforced.

The Impreza 555 rally cars wore gold-painted Speedline alloy wheels, initially with a 16-inch diameter and later with a 17-inch diameter. These wheels resembled the standard road-car alloys, but were in fact completely different. Tyres were always by Pirelli. From the beginning, the cars had a heat-exchanger for the engine oil, and a special six-speed gearbox developed by Prodrive. This was based on the earlier STI manual gearbox, but was a constant-mesh type with many internal components manufactured by racing-transmission specialists Hewland. Later versions of this gearbox could be used as a conventional manual or as a semi-automatic, and featured buttons on the steering wheel. The gears were changed by means of electronics and servos; compressed air moved the floor-mounted gear lever with the changes so that it was always in the right position on the gate if the driver wanted to go back to full manual control.

The cars had ventilated disc brakes all round, increased in size to 14 inches with the 17-inch wheels, and were provided with a water-spray facility to keep the intercooler temperature down on fast tarmac stages. They had mechanical locking differentials for the front and rear wheels, and the centre differential could be locked electronically. They were also ballasted to give them a weight distribution of 55 per cent at the front and 45 per cent at the rear. These proportions gave the best handling balance.

1993 SEASON

Events
1000 Lakes (Finland), 27–29 August
RAC (Rally GB), 21–24 November

Drivers
Ari Vatanen/Bruno Berglund
Markku Alén/Ilkka Kivimaki
Colin McRae/Derek Ringer

Cars
L555 BAT
L555 STE

The Impreza made its rally debut on the 1000 Lakes Rally in August 1993. Car number 5 was piloted by guest driver Markku Alén.

Colin McRae was leading the 1993 RAC Rally when radiator damage forced him to retire.

Podium Finishes
Finland: Vatanen 2nd

Overall Results
Subaru 3rd in WRC Manufacturers' Championship (including results with Legacy rally cars)

The Prodrive-prepared Impreza rally cars made their debut mid-way through the 1993 World Rally Championship. The team had campaigned Prodrive-prepared Legacy models in the first stages, and had already achieved some very respectable results: Markku Alén was fourth in the Rallye Portugal, and Colin McRae won the Rally New Zealand, the eighth event of the season. The Group A Legacy cars would also contest the Rally Australia later in the season, because cars and crews were already in place after the New Zealand event. Two Legacy Turbos would also contest the RAC Rally in Great Britain in November, but their days in the Subaru rally team were otherwise over.

Keen watchers of the rally scene expected the Impreza's debut some time during 1993, as the car had been homologated for WRC events on 1st April that year. In fact, its first appearance was in Finland, towards the end of August, at the long-established event then still usually known as the 1000 Lakes Rally. Two cars were entered: car number 2 was to be driven by Ari Vatanen while car number 5 was given to guest driver Markku Alén. Regular team driver Colin McRae was doing well in the Asia-Pacific Championship at the time, so he remained out East to compete in a Malaysian event, which he won for Subaru.

Alén was out of the Finnish event very quickly, crashing on the very first stage after entering a corner too fast. He was not invited to drive for Subaru again. However, Vatanen's car performed superbly, and on stage 26 was in the lead. Unfortunately, the light cluster fitted for the next special stage caused airflow problems; rain got into the heater system and the windscreen kept misting up. Constantly clearing the screen with a glove cost Vatanen valuable time and lost him the lead, with the result that the first place went to a Toyota Celica.

It was none the less a mightily impressive near-miss for the Impreza. Vatanen finished in second place, just two seconds behind the winner. With a podium finish on its first rally outing, the new Impreza was clearly about to make waves.

There was just one more event for the new cars in their first season: the RAC Rally in Britain at the end of November. Competing alongside a pair of Legacy Turbos, Colin McRae in car number 2 and Ari Vatanen in car number 5 once again demonstrated that the new Impreza was going to be a force in rallying. McRae won no fewer than nine stages and was leading on the third day of the event before being forced to retire after his radiator was holed and the engine overheated. Vatanen set fastest time on three stages, lost time with a brief 'off', and ultimately finished in fifth place.

1994 SEASON

Events
Monte Carlo, 22–27 January
Portugal, 1–4 March
Kenya (Safari), 31 March–4 April (Group N)
Tour de Corse (Corsica), 5–7 May
Greece (Acropolis), 29–31 May
Argentina, 30 June–2 July
New Zealand, 29–31 July
1000 Lakes (Rally Finland), 26–28 August
San Remo, 9–12 October
RAC (Rally GB), 20–23 November

Drivers
Carlos Sainz/Luis Moya
Patrick Njiru/Abdul Sidi (Group N only)
Richard Burns/Robert Reid (Group N and Group A)
Peter Bourne/Tony Sircombe
Colin McRae/Derek Ringer

Cars

L555 BAT	L555 STE
L555 REP	M555 STE
L555 SRT	

Podium Finishes
Monte Carlo: Sainz 3rd
Tour de Corse: Sainz 2nd
Acropolis: Sainz 1st
Argentina: Sainz 2nd
New Zealand: McRae 1st
1000 Lakes: Sainz 3rd
San Remo: Sainz 2nd
RAC: McRae 1st

Carlos Sainz had joined the team for 1994, and is seen here at the Portuguese event in March.

Colin McRae started the season badly, but ended it in triumph with victory on the RAC Rally.

Overall Results
Subaru 2nd in WRC Manufacturers' Championship
Sainz 2nd in WRC Drivers' Championship
McRae 4th in WRC Drivers' Championship

For 1994, the cars were modified with adjustable front differentials, and the Subaru team switched from Michelin to Pirelli tyres. The team was greatly strengthened by the recruitment of Carlos Sainz, twice WRC champion driver, who joined the team with his co-driver Luis Moya. It was a major coup that reflected the growing prestige of the SWRT. Sainz naturally assumed the position of number one driver, with McRae in the junior slot.

After third and second placings in Monte Carlo and Corsica, Sainz claimed the Impreza 555's first win at the Acropolis Rally in May. He then went on to claim two more second places, in Argentina and San Remo, plus a third place in Finland. McRae meanwhile had a dreadful start to the season. He crashed out on the Monte, retired after an engine fire in Portugal, crashed in Corsica, was excluded in Greece on a technicality that was not his fault, and crashed again in Argentina. But in New Zealand, where

he had won a year earlier, he drove the Impreza to victory. Subaru chose to rest him for the 1000 Lakes and San Remo events, but he then came back strongly on the RAC Rally and won again on his home turf.

The 1994 season was also notable for the Subaru debut of Richard Burns, with co-driver Robert Reid. Burns piloted a Group N car to seventh place in the Safari Rally, and had another turn behind the wheel with a Group A car on the RAC event. He did not finish the RAC, but he would be back.

1995 SEASON

Events
Monte Carlo, 21–26 January
Sweden, 10–12 February
Portugal, 8–10 March
Tour de Corse (Corsica), 3–5 May
New Zealand, 27–30 July
Australia, 15–18 September
Spain, 23–25 October
RAC (Rally GB), 19–22 November

Car number 4 in the 1995 Portugal Rally was driven by Carolos Sainz, who went on to win the event.

It was a nail-biting finish to the 1995 season, with Sainz and McRae tied for points at the start of the Network Q RAC Rally. McRae won, clinching the Drivers' Championship. He is seen here on the right, with the Scottish flag between him and co-driver Derek Ringer.

Drivers
Carlos Sainz/Luis Moya
Piero Liatti/Alex Alessandrini
Mats Jonsson/Johnny Johansson
Richard Burns/Robert Reid
Peter Bourne/Tony Sircombe
Colin McRae/Derek Ringer

Cars
L555 REP   M555 STE   L555 BAT

Podium Finishes
Monte Carlo: Sainz 1st
Portugal: Sainz 1st; McRae 3rd
New Zealand: McRae 1st
Australia: McRae 2nd
Spain: Sainz 1st; McRae 2nd; Liatti 3rd
RAC: McRae 1st; Sainz 2nd; Burns 3rd

Overall Results
Subaru 1st in WRC Manufacturers' Championship
McRae 1st in WRC Drivers' Championship

In theory, the cars that Subaru World Rally Team (SWRT) fielded for 1995 were the same ones they had used in 1994, although, in view of the fact that each one would have been extensively rebuilt after its last outing, any resemblance was probably purely coincidental! New FIA regulations in any case meant that they had been fitted with more restrictive turbocharger air intakes, and Prodrive had compensated for this by changing the camshafts and the compression ratio.

For 1995, Sainz remained the primary driver in car number 5, and McRae held the second slot in car number 4. Between them, these drivers claimed five wins in eight events for Subaru, winning the team its first Constructors' Championship title and netting the Drivers' Championship title for McRae. It was a massive success for the Japanese manufacturer.

SWRT fielded a third car in every one of those eight events. In New Zealand and the RAC Rally the driver was Richard Burns again, and he also drove a Group N Impreza on the Safari. In New Zealand, Sainz was out of action through injury, and so local driver Peter 'Possum' Bourne stepped in, with Tony Sircombe as co-driver. The same pair drove the third car in the Australian event. Piero Liatti drove the third car in the Monte and in Spain, with Luis Moya in the co-driver's seat. Finally, two-time Swedish Rally champion Mats Jonsson took the third car in Sweden, with Johnny Johansson as co-driver.

Sainz won at Monte Carlo, but McRae crashed out. Sainz, McRae and Jonsson all had engine failure in Sweden and did not finish; all three cars had the same problem with blocked oil-pressure relief valves. In Portugal, Sainz won despite a crash, and McRae claimed third, while in Corsica Sainz, McRae and third driver Piero Liatti took fourth, fifth and sixth places respectively. New Zealand gave McRae his first win of the season, while Peter Bourne came seventh and Richard Burns retired with mechanical failure.

McRae came second in Australia, but Sainz retired when his radiator failed and Bourne was out after an accident. In Spain, the leading Toyotas were disqualified for a rule infringement and Subaru finished with Sainz, McRae and Liatti in 1-2-3. The team had instructed McRae to slow down on the final day, to allow Sainz to win his 'home' event; McRae was not best pleased with the order. The result in Spain left Sainz and McRae tied for championship points at the start of the last event, but it was McRae who won that event and the drivers' title. Sainz was close behind him in second, and Burns took third at Rally GB, giving Subaru another 1-2-3 finish.

What Were They Called?

Subaru identified its first-generation Impreza WRC cars by names which incorporated digits identifying the rally season for which they were built. The list is as follows:

1997 season: WRC97
1998 season: WRC98
1999 season: WRC99
2000 season: WRC2000

Prodrive used different names for some of these cars, as follows:

1999 season: S5
2000 season: S6

The 1996 Catalunya event was another nail-biting event, with a close fight for points between McRae and Piero Liatti. McRae, in car number 1, came out on top…just.

McRae won in Greece, too, and the points all added up to give Subaru the constructors' title for the second year running.

1996 SEASON

Events
Sweden, 9–11 February
Kenya (Safari), 5–7 April
Indonesia, 10–12 May
Acropolis (Greece), 2–4 June
Argentina, 4–6 July
1000 Lakes (Finland), 23–26 August
Australia, 15–18 September
San Remo, 13–16 October
Spain, 4–6 November

Drivers
Piero Liatti/Mario Ferfoglia (Sweden only)
Piero Liatti/Fabrizia Pons
Colin McRae/Derek Ringer
Kenneth Eriksson/Staffan Parmander
Didier Auriol/Bernard Occelli
Hideyaki Miyoshi/Tinu Khan (Group N only)
Patrick Njiru/Rick Matthews (Group N only)

Cars
L555 SRT   N555 SRT
N1 WRC   N555 WRC   N555 BAT

Podium Finishes
Sweden: McRae 3rd
Safari: Eriksson 2nd
Indonesia: Liatti 2nd
Acropolis: McRae 1st
Argentina: Eriksson 3rd
Australia: Eriksson 2nd
San Remo: McRae 1st
Spain: McRae 1st

Overall Results
Subaru 1st in WRC Manufacturers' Championship
McRae 2nd in WRC Drivers' Championship

There was a reshuffle of drivers in the Subaru team for 1996. Carlos Sainz had yielded to a tempting offer to drive for Ford, and so Colin McRae automatically moved up to the number one spot. The number two driver was Kenneth Eriksson, while Piero Liatti drove the third car.

The season opened with the Swedish event, and Subaru entered four cars. The 1994 World Champion Didier

Auriol was given a turn in the number 3 car, but finished a disappointing tenth, and did not drive for Subaru again. McRae managed third place, with Eriksson fifth and Liatti 12th. In the Safari, Eriksson was second, McRae fourth, and Liatti fifth. Indonesia – a new event in the WRC calendar – saw McRae and Eriksson both retiring after accidents, leaving Liatti to finish second.

In the Acropolis, the Imprezas wore a new type of Pirelli tyre, and the improvement showed. McRae picked up his first win, despite propshaft bearing failure at the very last minute, with Liatti and Eriksson fourth and fifth respectively. Argentina saw Eriksson third and Liatti fifth, but McRae now embarked on a run of bad luck, crashing out of both Argentina and Finland; Liatti did not compete in Finland, but Eriksson managed a fifth place. Australia saw Eriksson 2nd, McRae 4th and Liatti 7th. McRae won in San Remo and Eriksson was fifth; Liatti retired with electrical problems. Then came Catalunya, which witnessed an exciting head-to-head contest between team-mates McRae and Liatti: McRae won with Liatti just 7 seconds behind him. Eriksson came home in seventh place.

Thanks to consistent podium finishes, Subaru retained the constructors' title, but this year McRae lost the drivers' title to Tommi Makinen.

1997–2000

For the 1997 season, the FIA introduced new regulations for the World Rally Championship. Out went the Group A regulations, and in came the new World Rally Car regulations. The intention was to ease the development of new cars and to encourage more manufacturers into the competition. Events became shorter. The event rotation system used for the previous three rally seasons was dropped, but one important new rule stipulated that manufacturers registered for the championship would be required to contest every rally designated as a WRC event.

In many ways, teams were given greater latitude than before. The earlier requirement for a minimum production run of 25,000 cars to homologate the rally machines was removed, although rally cars still had to be based on a production model. There was considerable room for deviation from the production specification, though: engines, intercoolers, suspension geometry, vehicle width and aerodynamics could all now be altered.

The 1997 WRC rules demanded some changes to the cars, and Subaru decided to use two-door models. This is Colin McRae on his way to a win in Australia.

Piero Liatti, the second Subaru driver for 1997, in action at the San Remo event in October. He finished second to McRae.

1997 SEASON

Events
Monte Carlo, 19–22 January
Sweden, 7–10 February
Kenya (Safari), 1–3 March
Portugal, 23–26 March
Catalunya (Spain), 14–16 April
Tour de Corse (Corsica), 5–7 May
Argentina, 22–24 May
Acropolis (Greece), 8–10 June
New Zealand, 2–5 August
1000 Lakes (Finland), 29–31 August
Indonesia, 19–21 September
San Remo, 12–15 October
Australia, 30 October– 2 November
RAC (Rally GB), 23–25 November

Drivers
Piero Liatti/Fabrizia Pons
Colin McRae/Nicky Grist
Kenneth Eriksson/Staffan Parmander

Cars
P2 WRC   P11 WRC

P3 WRC	P12 WRC
P4 WRC	P14 WRC
P5 WRC	P16 WRC
P7 WRC	P17 WRC
P8 WRC	P18 WRC
P9 WRC	P19 WRC
P10 WRC	P982 YWL

Podium Finishes
Monte Carlo: Liatti 1st
Sweden: Eriksson 1st
Safari: McRae 1st
Spain: Liatti 2nd
Tour de Corse: McRae 1st
Argentina: McRae 2nd; Eriksson 3rd
New Zealand: Eriksson 1st
Indonesia: Eriksson 3rd
San Remo: McRae 1st
Australia: McRae 1st
RAC: McRae 1st

Overall Results
Subaru 1st in WRC Manufacturers' Championship
McRae 2nd in WRC Drivers' Championship

Prodrive made full use of the new latitude allowed by the WRC regulations. They started work on the WRC97 car in the first quarter of 1996, creating the new rally machine out of the two-door or coupé body shell that had become available (under the Retna name) on the Japanese market in January 1995. The reason was simple: the two-door shell was considerably lighter than the four-door type. The WRC97 car was announced in public in April 1996, just under nine months before it would first see action on the opening event of the 1997 season. Homologation was completed on 1st January, a couple of weeks before that event.

From the outside, the two-door body was the most obvious new feature, but a closer look revealed a larger air intake in the front apron, with angled sides. The wings, too, were wider to cover wider tracks, and there was a bigger rear wing spoiler to increase downforce at high speed. These modifications were the work of Peter Stevens, who had earlier been with Lotus and from 2000 would take charge of MG Rover's design studios. Less noticeable at first glance was the relocation of the single big-bore exhaust outlet, from the left to the right.

Mechanically, the car had been completely overhauled. The engine had been moved 25mm (1in) rearwards to improve weight distribution, and its camshafts, cylinder ports and combustion chambers had all been redesigned. A lighter crankshaft was accompanied by a revised turbocharger and manifold design, and better cooling; a larger intercooler was also fitted, and now sat closer to the front of the engine. Power was quoted as 300bhp at 5500rpm, with maximum torque of 347lb ft at 4000 rpm.

The wider tracks increased overall width to 1770mm (69.9in), and the car scaled at 1230kg (2706lb), which was dead on the minimum required under the latest FIA regulations. There were active front and centre differentials with a mechanical LSD at the rear, and the gearbox was a six-speed built by Prodrive. A great deal had changed inside the car, too. Large areas of the dashboard were now made of lightweight carbon fibre, and, instead of the analogue instruments familiar from the road cars, there was a large monitor screen directly ahead of the driver.

As far as the drivers were concerned, Colin McRae was again the team leader, driving car number 3. Derek Ringer had left the team, apparently against his will, and Welshman Nicky Grist took over the co-driver's seat in McRae's car. Car number 4 was normally in the hands of Piero Liatti as the number two driver, again with Fabrizia Pons as co-

driver, but for some events the number 4 car was handled by Kenneth Eriksson and Staffan Parmander. On the RAC rally in November, there was a three-car entry, with Eriksson in the number 4 car and Liatti in car number 8.

Once again, the Subaru team had a terrific season. Liatti opened the proceedings well by winning the Monte – the new car's first outing, too. McRae was among the top five drivers but hit black ice and crashed out of the event. In Sweden, McRae again spun out of the event, but Liatti shrugged off the gearbox trouble that had slowed him on the first day and came through to win again. The Safari was good, too, with a much-deserved win for McRae, although Eriksson did not finish, after losing a wheel. In Portugal, engine failures put both McRae and Eriksson out of contention.

Both McRae and Liatti drove strongly on the Catalunya event, but a puncture on the second day knocked McRae back to fourth place, while Liatti eventually had to settle for second – still a good finish. Then came Corsica, with a win for McRae and a good fifth placing for Liatti. Argentina, too, ended with the Subaru team taking two of the podium places, but McRae's second and Eriksson's third had been hard won: McRae's car developed transmission and steering problems, and Eriksson also had gearbox trouble. More steering problems put both the works Imprezas out of contention in Greece after a strong start. Then engine failure put McRae out of the New Zealand rally, leaving Eriksson to storm ahead and finish in first place.

Both Eriksson and McRae retired from the 1000 Lakes event with failed camshaft belt pulleys, and in Indonesia an accident on the second day put McRae out of the running. Eriksson, however, pressed on to a strong third place. The rest of the season was superb. McRae came first in San Remo, with Liatti second. In Australia, McRae won again, although Eriksson did not finish; and on the RAC Rally McRae was again the winner, with Liatti finishing 7th and engine trouble putting Eriksson's car out of the running. Unfortunately for Subaru's championship points, it was Eriksson and not Liatti who had been their second nominated driver.

Yet those eight victories in 14 rallies and multiple podium finishes all added up, and Subaru finished the season as clear winners of the Constructors' Championship for the third year running. McRae had to be content with second place in the drivers' rankings, beaten to the title by Mitsubishi's Tommi Makinen and by just a single point.

Colin McRae airborne in the WRC98 car on his way to victory in the 1998 Australian event.

1998 SEASON

Events
Monte Carlo, 18–21 January
Sweden, 5–8 February
Kenya (Safari), 27 February– 2 March
Portugal, 22–25 March
Spain, 19–22 April
Tour de Corse (Corsica), 3–6 May
Argentina, 20–23 May
Acropolis (Greece), 5–9 June
New Zealand, 25–28 July
1000 Lakes (Finland), 21–23 August
San Remo, 10–14 October
Australia, 5–8 November
RAC (Rally GB), 21–23 November

Drivers
Piero Liatti/Fabrizia Pons
Colin McRae/Nicky Grist
Kenneth Eriksson/Staffan Parmander
Jarno Kytolehto/Arto Kapanen
Ari Vatanen/ Fabrizia Pons

Cars
P7 WRC   R11 WRC

The snow of the Monte Carlo was a huge contrast to the dry heat of Australia; McRae was put out of the 1998 event by engine failure.

P14 WRC	R12 WRC
R7 WRC	R14 WRC
R8 WRC	R15 WRC
R9 WRC	R17 WRC
R10 WRC	R19 WRC

Podium Finishes
Monte Carlo: McRae 3rd
Portugal: McRae 1st
Tour de Corse: McRae 1st; Liatti 3rd
Acropolis: McRae 1st
San Remo: Liatti 2nd; McRae 3rd

Overall Results
Subaru 3rd in WRC Manufacturers' Championship
McRae 3rd in WRC Drivers' Championship

The WRC98 car was very much an evolution of the successful WRC97 type, with all three differentials now active types controlled by computer, plus an electronic throttle. The new hardware performed as expected, but the season was dogged by mechanical failures.

Colin McRae remained lead driver, and this year Piero Liatti stepped into the number two position. Kenneth Eriksson did drive for Subaru in the Swedish event, but then left to join the new Hyundai WRC team. Subaru ran

New to the Subaru team in 1998, Juha Kankkunen was the winning driver in the Finland Rally.

two cars in most events, but there were three in Sweden and on the RAC Rally. Guest crews were Jarmo Kytöle-hto and Arto Kapanen on the 1000 Lakes (where they came a disappointing eighth), and Colin McRae's brother Alister with David Senior on the RAC event (where they did not finish).

McRae won in Portugal, Corsica and Greece, the Portuguese win being particularly narrow with the Impreza just 2.1 seconds ahead of Carlos Sainz's new Toyota Corolla. In New Zealand he came a disappointing fifth, and then a courageous fifth in Argentina after he had severely damaged his car's suspension. Engine failure prevented him from finishing in the Monte, the Safari, in Australia and on the RAC. At Catalunya, he withdrew in disgust when the latest tyres proved inadequate for the job, and on the 1000 Lakes he crashed out of the event. All was clearly not well, and it was no big surprise when he announced that he would be leaving Subaru to join the Ford team for 1999. Even so, to finish with third place in the Drivers' Championship for 1998 was no disgrace.

Liatti had to content himself with an almost equally disappointing season. He finished fourth on the Monte, 9th in Sweden, 6th in Portugal and 6th again in Argentina, on the Acropolis and in New Zealand. His only podium finishes were a second place in San Remo and a third in Corsica. Like McRae, he had suffered mechanical problems, and had not finished on the Safari (where his engine had failed), in Spain (where he crashed), or in Australia.

It had been a bad year. Subaru dropped to third place in the Constructors' Championship, British American Tobacco announced that they would not sponsor the team for 1999, and Subaru had lost its top driver to a rival team. Piero Liatti also announced that he was off, to drive for SEAT in 1999.

1999 SEASON

Events
Monte Carlo, 17–21 January
Sweden, 11–14 February
Kenya (Safari), 25–28 February
Portugal, 23–26 March
Spain, 19–21 April
Tour de Corse (Corsica), 7–9 May
Argentina, 22–25 May
Acropolis (Greece), 6–9 June
New Zealand, 15–18 July
1000 Lakes (Finland), 20–22 August
China, 16–19 September
San Remo, 11–13 October
Australia, 4–7 November
RAC (Rally GB), 21–23 November

Drivers
Juha Kankkunen/Juha Repo
Bruno Thiry/Stéphane Prévot
Richard Burns/Robert Reid

Cars
P7 WRC	S10 SRT
R9 WRC	T11 SRT
R15 WRC	T12 SRT
S6 SRT	T14 SRT
S7 SRT	T15 SRT
S8 SRT	-005 (China only)
S9 SRT	-006 (China only)

Richard Burns, back with Subaru for 1999, pictured on his way to victory in Australia. He finished the season placed second in the drivers' championship.

Podium Finishes
Monte Carlo: Kankkunen 2nd
Argentina: Kankkunen 1st; Burns 2nd
Acropolis: Burns 1st
New Zealand: Kankkunen 2nd
1000 Lakes: Kankkunen 1st; Burns 2nd
China: Burns 2nd
Australia: Burns 1st
RAC: Burns 1st

Overall Results
Subaru 2nd in WRC Manufacturers' Championship
Burns 2nd in WRC Drivers' Championship

Ten new cars were built for 1999, all finished in the traditional Subaru blue but this time with large Subaru star logos on their flanks in place of the 555 emblems. All the funding now came from Japan. Prodrive had developed a Formula One-style electronically controlled sequential gear-change system, with a paddle shift, but this was not used before the Catalunya event. The cars also had new roll cages that were both lighter and stronger than before. The air scoops were blanked off now that the intercoolers were in the nose, and there were bigger air outlet vents on the bonnet. The cars also had a new roof vent above the windscreen.

The crews were all new. The most experienced of Subaru's new drivers was Juha Kankkunen, four times World Champion and newly recruited from Ford. Alongside him was Richard Burns, returning to the Subaru fold from Mitsubishi, and for the first half of the season, Bruno Thiry also handled a number of Impreza entries. Unfortunately Thiry did not achieve the results that both he and Subaru wanted.

Both crews and cars took time to settle down, and technical problems meant that the team struggled before the seventh round, in Argentina. There were three-car entries for the first five rounds. These were then reduced to two and Bruno Thiry left the team in mid-season. However, the early events had not been entirely without good news, with Kankkunen coming second in the Monte, and, from May and the Argentina rally, things began to pick up. Kankkunen won in Argentina and then in Finland during August. Richard Burns showed his true mettle with second places in Argentina, Finland and China, and victories on the Acropolis in June, on the Australian event and on the season-closing RAC Rally. Podium places in seven out of the later eight rounds, with five wins including three 1-2 finishes – that was more like it.

Subaru finished one place further up the manufacturers' table in second place this year, a mere four points behind Toyota. Burns' three victories helped him to second place in the drivers' tables, with Kankkunen coming fourth.

2000 SEASON

Events
Monte Carlo, 20–22 January
Sweden, 10–13 February
Kenya (Safari), 25–27 February
Portugal, 16–19 March
Spain, 31 March – 2 April
Argentina, 11–14 May
Acropolis (Greece), 9–11 June
New Zealand, 13–16 July
1000 Lakes (Finland), 18–20 August

Behind the Wheel: The Subaru WRC drivers, 1993–2000

Markku ALÉN

Markku Alén drove just twice for the Subaru World Rally Team, once at the wheel of a Legacy in 1990 and again on the Impreza's rally debut in Finland in 1993. He was the son of a former Finnish ice-racing champion who had established a formidable reputation as a hard-charging rally driver from his first major event in 1973. Alén subsequently drove for Fiat, Ford and Lancia. After a year with Toyota in 1992, he divided his 1993 season between that company and Subaru. However, his front-line rallying career was effectively over, although he subsequently drove touring cars for Alfa Romeo and competed in the French Trophée Andros ice-racing series in 1996–1997.

Didier AURIOL

Frenchman Auriol guested only once behind the wheel of an Impreza WRC, in 1996. By this time he was already a world-class driver, having been World Champion with Toyota in 1994. He was one of the world's leading rally drivers throughout the 1990s, but left WRC competition at the end of 2003 after a stint with Skoda.

Peter 'Possum' BOURNE

New Zealander Peter Bourne earned his nickname of 'Possum' after crashing his mother's car while trying to avoid a possum in the road. He entered WRC events in 1983 with a Subaru RX, and was always closely associated with the marque, joining the SWRT for a number of events in the mid-1990s. He won the Asia-Pacific Rally Championship three times and was Australian Rally Champion for seven consecutive years. He died after a collision on the road in 2003, while on his way to an event. At the time, he had just re-entered world rallying, driving a Group N Impreza in the Production World Rally Championship.

Richard BURNS

British driver Burns started amateur rallying as a teenager and rapidly established himself as a formidable talent. In 1992 he became British National Champion at the wheel of a Subaru Legacy, and a year later was invited to join the Subaru team, driving a Legacy in the British Championship. He remained with Subaru for 1994 and 1995, as third driver with Colin McRae and Carlos Sainz.
From 1996 Burns was with Mitsubishi Ralliart and in 1998 won his first WRC event. For 1999 he was back with Subaru,

taking the place vacated by McRae. After a superb season in 2001, he became World Champion, but was poached from Subaru for 2002 by Peugeot after a messy legal battle. Success eluded him here, and he was ready to drive for Subaru again in 2004 when he was taken ill. The diagnosis was a malignant brain tumour, and Burns sadly died in 2005.

Kenneth ERIKSSON

Swede Kenneth Eriksson had plenty of rally experience before he joined the Subaru team in 1996. He had been Group A Champion in 1986, and was a key member of the Mitsubishi team by 1995. His speciality was gravel rallies. From 1999 he was with Hyundai, moving to Skoda in 2002 but bowing out of WRC competition at the end of the year.

Simon JEAN-JOSEPH

Jean-Joseph was born in Martinique and made his rally debut in local events 1989. 'Jean-Jo' was several times Martinique champion and in 1997 won the French amateur rally championship in a Group A Impreza. He guested for Subaru just once, in 2000 on the Tour de Corse. He subsequently became European Rally Champion in 2004 but gave up rally driving for a time in 2008 after a boating accident. In 2011, he was back behind the wheel for the French championship.

Mats JONSSON

Swedish driver Jonsson was a regular in the WRC between 1984 and 1993. He drove for Opel from 1987–1989, and won the Swedish Rally as a privateer twice, in 1992 and 1993. He guested for Subaru just once, in 1995. He has continued to enter rallies as a privateer.

Juha KANKKUNEN

Kankkunen's WRC career lasted from 1983 to 2002, during which time he won 23 world rallies and four Driver's Championship titles. From 1983 he was with Toyota, then from 1986 Peugeot. He shuttled between Lancia and Toyota and then joined Ford in 1997. He moved to Subaru for 1999 and 2000, and subsequently drove part-time for Hyundai before retiring in 2002.

Jarmo KYTÖLEHTO

Finnish driver Kytölehto began rallying in 1988 and driving in WRC events in 1991. He had driven for Opel, Mitsubishi,

Nissan and Ford before being asked to drive an Impreza on the 1000 Lakes Rally in Finland in 1998. He subsequently earned drives with Vauxhall and Hyundai.

Piero LIATTI

Piero Liatti began his WRC career as a privateer, driving a Lancia Delta Integrale, and then a Subaru. The Italian's skill on tarmac rallies impressed Prodrive, who signed him for the Subaru works team between 1995 and 1998. Liatti moved on to SEAT in 1999, and has subsequently driven for Ford, Hyundai and Peugeot.

Colin McRAE

The success of Scottish-born Colin McRae made a major contribution to British interest in the Subaru World Rally Team in the 1990s. McRae came from a rallying family; his father was a five-times British Rally Champion, and his brother Alister also became a noted rally driver. Colin McRae became British Rally Champion in 1991 and 1992, and was selected for the Subaru World Rally Team in 1993, driving a Group A Legacy. He won his first WRC rally in a Legacy at the Rally New Zealand that year. This was also the first rally win for the newly formed Subaru World Rally Team.

For 1994, McRae switched to the new Impreza rally car, and that season for Subaru confirmed him as a major talent. In 1995 he became the first Briton and the youngest driver ever to win the World Rally Championship drivers' title. For the next three years he was the team's lead driver, but in 1999 he moved to the Ford rally team. In 2003, he moved again to join Citroën, but this would be his last season in WRC events. He later competed in both the Le Mans 24 Hours event and the Paris-Dakar Rally.

Colin McRae was tragically killed in a helicopter accident in September 2007, aged just 39. The McRae Vision Charity still honours his name.

Markko MÄRTIN

Märtin was an Estonian driver who had driven for Toyota and Ford before joining Subaru for the 2000 rallying season. He stayed for 2001 before rejoining Ford. A move to Peugeot in 2005 ended in tragedy when Märtin's car hit a tree, killing co-driver Michael Park. Understandably shaken, Märtin retired from WRC driving, but has since made a limited return to competitive rallying and in 2008 was signed as the official test driver for the Subaru team.

Patrick NJIRU

Kenyan Patrick NJIRU drove regularly for the Subaru World Rally Team between 1983 and 2002, when he retired from competitive racing. With the Imprezas, his role was always to pilot a car in the demanding Safari rally, where his experience was unrivalled among other Subaru drivers. He drove the Impreza in both Group A and Group N forms.

Carlos SAINZ

The Spanish driver Carlos Sainz began rallying in 1980 and was WRC World Drivers' Champion while with Toyota in 1990 and 1992. He joined Subaru in 1995 and subsequently drove for Toyota and Citroën. His last rally was the 2005 Acropolis. He subsequently became involved with Volkswagen for the Dakar Rally, and was asked to join the Volkswagen Polo WRC project for 2013.

Petter SOLBERG

Norwegian Petter Solberg was a local rallycross champion before entering his first rally in 1995. From 1999, he was signed up for Ford, but in 2000 joined Subaru where he became the mainstay of the team until Subaru pulled out of the WRC at the end of 2008. Solberg subsequently had a successful career as a privateer driving Citroëns before joining the Ford team in 2012.

Bruno THIRY

Belgian driver Thiry began as an amateur in 1981 and quickly proved himself in the Belgian Rally Championship. He joined Ford in 1994 as a WRC driver, and was with Subaru during 1999 as third driver. He has subsequently driven for Skoda, Peugeot and Citroën.

Ari VATANEN

Finnish rally driver Ari Vatanen was already an experienced veteran when he joined Subaru, in 1992. His first WRC drive had been in Finland in 1974, and from 1977 he had been a regular privateer WRC contestant at the wheel of a Ford Escort RS1800. During the 1980s he drove for Peugeot, returning to the sport after a serious accident in Argentina in 1985 nearly claimed his life. Between 1989 and 1990 he was with Mitsubishi Ralliart, and in 1993 it was Vatanen who drove the Impreza rally car to second place on its debut event in Finland. He briefly returned to a works Impreza for the Rally of Great Britain in 1998, which marked his 100th WRC event. Since 1999, he has become involved in politics.

The Cyprus event in 2000 was not one of Subaru's more successful events; Richard Burns in car number 3 came fourth after recurrent engine problems.

Petter Solberg joined the Subaru team in September 2000, and quickly got into his stride. He drove car number 17 at the Australian event in November.

Cyprus, 8–10 September
Tour de Corse (Corsica), 29 September – 1 October
San Remo, 20–22 October
Australia, 9–12 November
RAC (Rally GB), 23–26 November

Drivers
Juha Kankkunen/Juha Repo
Richard Burns/Robert Reid
Simon Jean-Joseph/Jack Boyère
Petter Solberg/Phil Mills
Markko Märtin/Michael Park

Cars

R20 WRC	W19 SRT
S10 SRT	W20 SRT
T14 SRT	W21 SRT
T15 SRT	W22 SRT
T16 SRT	W23 SRT
W17 SRT	W24 SRT
W18 SRT	W25 SRT

Podium Finishes
Monte Carlo: Kankkunen 3rd
Safari: Burns 1st; Kankkunen 2nd

A Preserved WRC Impreza

Prodrive, the builders of the Subaru World Rally Team cars, have preserved in their Heritage Centre the car that was driven by Colin McRae with Nicky Grist in the 1997 championship series. In that year, McRae drove to victory in no fewer than five events. The car has been completely restored by Prodrive, using all original parts and a restoration team comprised of mechanics, designers and engineers who worked on the car in 1997.

Prodrive lent the car to Mike LeCaplain of *Classic Car Weekly* for a brief drive, and he published his report in the magazine's issue of 10 August 2011:

Driving a Subaru World Rally car is a bit like experiencing the world's greatest rollercoaster; it's incredibly loud, frightening, and awe-inspiringly quick.

Climb inside and you'll find Impreza WRC97 as Colin McRae left it, with Sparco racing wheel, digital displays and swathes of carbon fibre. A huge roll cage encases the driver, making things a bit cramped, but the bucket seats are surprisingly comfortable. There's no ignition key so the driver has to initiate a series of pumps and fans to prime the engine. The car is thunderously loud and a few dabs of the throttle is all that's needed to leave your teeth rattling as the 300bhp unit warms up.

At low speeds the road legal WRC97 is cumbersome and difficult, but get it onto the open road and you're in for one of the most incredible driving experiences of your life.

There's a whopping 347lb ft of torque available at 4000rpm and the Impreza will comfortably hit 60mph from a standstill in just three seconds.

Bury the throttle and your body's pinned to the back of the seat as the four-wheel drive system and 16-inch Pirelli tyres find traction and launch the Impreza down the road like a wayward missile. Turbo lag is non-existent and, with short gear ratios, the drive can crack through the six-speed manual 'box with ease to reach terrifying speeds.

Pushed to the edge the WRC97 is all encompassing and lets the driver feel completely at one with it. Admittedly a firm hand is needed to keep the Impreza on the straight and narrow as the steering wheel writhes under full throttle and the Impreza jolts from side to side as uneven road surfaces and pot holes attempt to throw it off the road. However, all of that becomes second nature as the car's breath-taking performance and grip inspire the driver to push further and harder.

Make no mistake; this is a brutal machine, with a deafening engine roar and spine-breaking ride. But if you can suffer all of that then you'll be transported to an adrenaline-filled heaven.

Portugal: Burns 1st
Spain: Burns 2nd
Argentina: Burns 1st
Acropolis: Kankkunen 3rd
Australia: Burns 2nd
RAC: Burns 1st

Overall Results
Subaru 3rd in WRC Manufacturers' Championship
Burns 2nd in WRC Drivers' Championship
Subaru started the 2000 season with a further 10 WRC99-specification cars, and did not introduce the new WRC2000 model until the Portugal rally in March. The new car looked little different from the old, but had been extensively redesigned under Prodrive's project engineer, Christian Loriaux. Weight had been saved, and much of that which could not be saved had been pushed lower in the car to improve stability. The inner body shell, roll cage and fuel tank had all been redesigned, the suspension light-ened, and the rear cross-member modified. On the engine, the locations of the turbocharger, manifolds and ducting had all changed, and the intercooler had now been mounted above the radiator right in the nose of the car.

It was to be a tremendous season for Richard Burns, but for Juha Kankkunen it proved a frustrating one. Kankkunen managed third on the Monte and the Acropolis, and second in Sweden, but he was clearly becoming increasingly discontented and decided to leave the team at the end of the season. Burns, meanwhile, was getting into his stride. He kicked off a season of four wins with victory in Sweden, and followed this up with first places in Portugal, Argentina and on the RAC Rally. His reward was second place in the drivers' rankings again. By the time of the Corsican rally at the end of September, SWRT was already looking to the future, and three additional crews entered the season's four remaining events. Petter Solberg and co-driver Phil Mills would stay the course; Stéphane Jean-Joseph and Markko Martin guested only for one rally each.

CHAPTER 5

SPECIAL EDITIONS OF THE FIRST GENERATION CARS

Clever marketing has been a part of the Impreza Turbo story right from the beginning, and Subaru has always released special-edition models at intervals to ensure that interest and demand remain at a high level. These special-edition models have particular appeal because they have unique features – or, at least, features that were unique when they were new – and because their numbers are strictly limited. Special editions have been a feature of Japanese car marketing on the domestic market; with the Impreza Turbo, Subaru has successfully carried this over on to the world stage.

The special editions have differed from country to country, to suit market conditions. These differences give them a particular interest for some enthusiasts and in the UK, for example, some hardcore Impreza enthusiasts have imported examples of Japanese special editions simply because they are different from the cars regularly found in the UK.

The Impreza is a Japanese car, and it is therefore arguable that the Japanese domestic market lies at the centre of the Impreza community, with the result that Japanese special editions should take centre stage. However, this book is written primarily for readers in the UK, and therefore it is the UK special editions that are given special prominence. The UK editions are also of particular interest because several of them were produced in-territory by Prodrive, Subaru's long-time partner in the preparation of the World Rally Championship cars.

Note that no cars were ever issued with the limited-edition number 13, as that number is considered to be unlucky. As a result, the highest-numbered car in a limited edition will always be numbered one above the total – for example, in a limited edition of 200 cars, the highest-numbered car will be number 201.

UK SPECIAL EDITIONS

Series McRae (1995)

200 Examples

The Series McRae edition was introduced in June 1995 to honour the achievement of the Subaru 555 World Rally team in winning the WRC, and of Colin McRae in particular for winning the drivers' title. Prodrive prepared these cars, re-tuning the engines to give better mid-range response, and modifying the suspension to give tighter handling. When new, the cars cost £22,999 on the road.

The 1995 Series McRae celebrated that year's WRC drivers' title for Subaru driver Colin McRae, seen here with the car. The '555 BAT' registration actually belonged to one of the rally cars.

Six That Got Away

In 1993, Subaru UK imported six Japanese-specification Type RS cars, which were the development models that eventually led to the stripped-out Japanese Type RA. They had turbocharged 2-litre engines, but were registered as 1.8GL models for reasons associated with UK car certification regulations.

Three cars went to Prodrive, and the other three remained with Subaru UK until they were eventually sold.

Bodywork:
Rally Blue micatallic paint.
Electric tilt-and-slide sunroof.
Special badges on front wings and tail panel.

Interior:
Recaro front seats.
Monogrammed Le Mans/Avus speckled cloth upholstery with open head restraints.
Dashboard and gear knob with imitation carbon fibre or wood.
Special-edition plaque on centre console, reading 'Series McRae by Prodrive' and bearing the car number.

Engine:
1994cc engine with 240bhp.
Uprated engine management system.
Prodrive exhaust silencer.
Ram-air filter.

Running gear:
Uprated springs, dampers, and anti-roll bars.
Gold-finished 16-inch 6.5J Speedline Safari eight-spoke alloy wheels.
Pirelli P-Zero tyres as original equipment.

Catalunya (1997)

200 Examples
The Catalunya edition was announced in March 1997 to honour Subaru's second WRC title in 1996, which was

The Prodrive WR Sport Conversion (1997)

Strictly speaking an authorized conversion rather than a special edition, the Prodrive WR Sport was announced at the Earls Court Motor Show in 1997. Performance was tested by Autocar magazine and revealed 0–60mph in 5.6 seconds and 0–100mph in 15.9 seconds, with a 227km/h (141mph) top speed. Without extras, the car was priced at £30,169.

Bodywork:
Side skirts and door mirrors in body colour.
Taller rear wing.
Optional metallic paint.
Optional electric sunroof.

Interior:
Recaro sports front seats
Three extra gauges above central air vents.
Optional CD player.
Optional air conditioning.

Engine:
1994cc engine, with 240bhp at 5600rpm and 240lb ft at 4000rpm.
Revised ECU.
Ramair air filter.
New exhaust.

Running gear:
Uprated springs and dampers.
Six-spoke Speedline 17-inch 7J alloys.
Pirelli P-Zero 205/45 VR 17 tyres as original equipment.
Optional Quickshift.

won at the Rally of Spain in Catalunya. The car cost £21,610 when new. (A similar car finished in Blue Mica was available in Italy.)

Bodywork:
Black Mica paint with red flecks.
Body-colour door mirrors.
Catalunya decals on front wings and tail panel.

The black Catalunya edition of 1997 celebrated Subaru's second WRC title, won in 1996.

Interior:
Recaro Sports front seats.
Black cloth upholstery with red highlights; black door trims.
Black floor mats with red edging and Catalunya logo.
Air conditioning standard.
Gear knob with red stitching.
Short rally-style gear lever with Quickshift.
Numbered gold Catalunya plaque.
Carbon-fibre-effect instrument surround.

Engine:
1994cc engine, with standard 208bhp and 214lb ft.

Running gear:
Standard suspension.
Gold-finish 15-inch 6J five-spoke wheels.

Terzo (1997)

333 Examples
The Terzo edition was introduced in April 1998 to honour Subaru's third WRC title in 1997 (terzo being Italian for 'third'). When new, it cost £22,995.

Bodywork:
Terzo Blue Mica paint.
Terzo badges on front wings and tail panel.

Interior:
Black upholstery with grey alcantara highlights.
Special carpets.
Numbered plaque.
Alarm as standard.
Air conditioning.

The Subaru team's third WRC championship was commemorated by the 1997 Terzo special edition.

Engine:
1994cc engine, with standard 208bhp and 214lb ft.

Running gear:
Standard suspension.
Gold-painted 16-inch alloys (standard pattern, with Bridgestone Potenza tyres).

22B (1998)

16 Examples
The 22B was a two-door coupé model and the only Impreza to be fitted with a 2.2-litre engine. It was announced in March 1998 to commemorate both the third consecutive WRC win and Subaru's own 40th anniversary as a car maker, with the date being traced back to the introduction of the 360 in 1958, not the original 1500 in 1954. There were 400 examples for the Japanese home market, and a further 25 for export.

Of the 25 export cars, 16 were sold in the UK during 1999 after being made to conform to UK regulations by Prodrive and passing Single Vehicle Approval requirements; they were strictly known as 22B-STI Type UK models. However, before the Prodrive cars were made available, an estimated 50 Japanese-market cars had already been imported to the UK privately!

The origin of the 22B name remains in dispute. Some authorities suggest that the '22' reflected the 2.2-litre engine, and the 'B' stood for Bilstein suspension (as it did with the Legacy Spec B). Others argue that 22B is a hexadecimal representation of the number 555 associated with British American Tobacco, and displayed on the rally cars.

Bodywork:
Sonic Blue Mica paint.
'Wide body' with flared wings based on WRC cars; overall width is 1770mm (69.7in).
Pink STI logo on grille.
Special vents on standard bonnet.
Special front bumper, inspired by WRC cars.
STI logos on front wings.
Unique adjustable rear wing spoiler.
Single exhaust with chromed tip.

Interior:
Upholstery in blue and black, with red STI logo embroidered on seat backs.
Three-spoke Nardi steering wheel with red stitching; no airbag.
Numbered limited-edition plaque on centre console.
Anti-reflection coating on dashboard.

There were just 16 examples of the 22B special edition for the UK ... at least, officially. Enthusiasts had already brought in a good number from Japan before these official releases.

Engine:

2212cc EJ22 engine with enlarged 96.9mm bore; 276bhp at 6000rpm, 268lb ft at 3200rpm. The cylinder block is closed-deck type (and comes from an EJ20G Version 3 engine, not an EJ22G as is commonly supposed), with a metal head gasket, an 8.0:1 compression ratio; IHI RHF 5B turbocharger, and a redline of 7900rpm rather than 8000rpm. There are forged pistons, sodium-filled exhaust valves, and hollow-stem inlet valves. The inlet manifold and heads come from the EJ20K Version 4 engine. The intercooler has a water spray.

Running gear:

Gearbox ratios as Japanese-market WRX Type R, but with shot-peened gears.
Twin-plate competition clutch, with one ceramic plate.
Variable Torque Distribution system.
Tracks widened by 10mm (0.4in) at front and 40mm (1.6in) at rear.
Suspension with forged aluminium lower control arms, uprated bushes and rose-jointed lateral links, front and rear.
Eibach springs and Bilstein inverted dampers.
Carbon-fibre front strut brace.
Brakes with red-painted calipers that have the Subaru name cast in and painted white.
Quicker steering with 13:1 ratio.
BBS Elektra 18-inch wheels with 8.5J rims, painted gold; 235/40 ZR 17 Pirelli P-Zero tyres.

RB5 (1999)

444 Examples

The RB5 was named in honour of Richard Burns' arrival on the WRC team, with 'RB' for his initials and the number 5 being that of the car he regularly drove. All examples had a solid rear bulkhead to add to body rigidity. The basic RB5 model cost £24,995, but most examples had the Prodrive Performance Pack, and were priced at £27,495.

Bodywork:

Blue Steel metallic paint (this colour was used elsewhere with the name Cool Grey).
120-watt PIAA rally lights.
RB5 decals on fog-light covers, front wings and tail panel.
STI-type rear spoiler.

The 1999 RB5 was one of two special editions in honour of Subaru team driver Richard Burns.

Interior:

Short-throw gearshift.
Black and blue part-suede upholstery.
Graphite centre-console finish.
Numbered special-edition plaque (numbers run to 449; numbers 013, 113, 213, 313 and 413 were not issued).
Air conditioning.

Engine:

1994cc engine, with 215bhp at 5600rpm and 214lb ft at 4000rpm in standard trim.
Prodrive Performance Pack cars with 240PS (237bhp) at 6000rpm and 350Nm (258lb ft) at 3500rpm.

Running gear:

Standard suspension.
17-inch Speedline alloy wheels.

Options:

Prodrive suspension package.

P1 (2000)

1000 Examples

The P1 was a special edition created for Subaru UK by Prodrive. It was introduced at the 1999 Earls Court

ABOVE, LEFT TO RIGHT: *Released in March 2000, the P1 edition was based on the two-door shell used for the 22B two years earlier. The car was prepared by Prodrive.*

Motor Show, but did not go on sale until March 2000. The car was supposedly intended to counter imports of high-performance Japanese Imprezas. It was based on the two-door coupé body shell with a solid rear bulkhead. The original plan was to build 500 examples, but the total was doubled to meet demand. The showroom cost was £31,500.

Bodywork:
Sonic Blue Mica paint.
Front spoiler with slotted lower lip and Hella driving lamps instead of fog lights.
Optional Hella gas-discharge spotlights.
Rear spoiler with P1 logo inserts.
Body-colour door mirrors, door handles, and sill extensions.
Impreza P1 badge on boot lid.
Green tinted glass.
Rear wiper.

Interior:
Prodrive front bucket seats.
Optional Recaro front bucket seats with electric adjustment.
Black, red and blue cloth upholstery with grey alcantara highlights.
Optional leather upholstery.

Grey alcantara on door trims.
Prodrive carpets.
Red stitching on steering wheel and gear knob.
White instrument faces.
Air conditioning.
Electric windows.
Twin airbags.
CD player.

Engine:
1994cc engine with 280PS (276bhp) at 6500rpm and 253lb ft at 4000rpm.
8.2:1 compression ratio.
Reprogrammed ECU (by Subaru).
Single catalytic converter instead of twin converters.
STI tailpipe.
Optional large-bore exhaust, with tailpipe stamped 'P1 (Prodrive)'.

Running gear:
Gear ratios 3.17:1, 1.88:1, 1.30:1, 0.97:1, 0.74:1; final drive 4.44:1.
WRX rear springs.
Uprated front and rear dampers.
Altered suspension geometry.
Carbon-fibre front strut brace.
ABS standard.

Optional uprated brakes with 326mm front discs and Alcon four-piston calipers.

10-spoke, 17-inch 7J OZ alloy wheels in gunmetal grey, with 205/45 ZR 17 tyres; Pirelli P-Zero as original equipment. Optional 18-inch OZ alloys in gold with 225/35 ZR 18 tyres.

JAPANESE SPECIAL EDITIONS

There was a degree of predictability about the Japanese special editions, as each new model-year brought the latest iteration of a familiar formula. Nevertheless, they were formidably effective in moving cars through the showrooms.

The model names for the Japanese domestic market initially seem complicated, but are easier to understand when broken down into their component parts:

WRX	the turbocharged Impreza
STI	the higher-performance editions prepared by STI
Version II	1996 model-year (autumn 1995 to summer 1996)
Version III	1997 model-year
Version IV	1998 model-year
Version V	1999 model-year
Version VI	2000 model-year
R	Racing
RA	Race Altered
V-Limited	Very Limited (in terms of numbers, although the description was not always strictly accurate!)

WRX STI Version II (1995)

500 Saloons, 100 Sports Wagons
The Version II STI-prepared cars were announced in August 1995 as limited editions. These were known as the 555 Pure Sports Sedan and the 555 Pure Sports Wagon, the number coming from the brand name of British American Tobacco which was sponsoring the Subaru World Rally Team.

Bodywork:
Sports Blue paint.
Roof vent (saloons only).
Bronze-tinted glass.
Rally-style mudflaps.
Optional WRC decal set.

Interior: As standard.

Engine:
Saloon: 1994cc engine with 275bhp at 6500rpm and 235lb ft at 4000rpm.
Sports Wagon: 1994cc engine with 260bhp at 6500rpm and 227lb ft at 4000rpm.
Both engines with red-painted inlet manifold.

Running gear:
16-inch wheels with Bridgestone tyres.
Optional gold-painted Speedline Electra S wheels.

WRX V-Limited (1996)

1000 Examples
This limited edition was introduced in February 1996. It was available in just three colours: Black Mica, Feather White and Sports Blue.

Bodywork:
Green-tinted glass.
Rear emblem in white, stating Subaru were 1995 WRC champions.

Interior:
Aluminium limited-edition plate with serial number.
STI-style seats with 1995 WRC Champions logo; black and grey upholstery.
Door trims in black and grey to match upholstery.

Engine:
1994cc engine with 260bhp.

Running gear:
Standard suspension.
ABS standard.
Gold STI five-spoke wheels.

WRX Type RA STI Version II V-Limited (1996)

555 Examples
This limited edition was introduced in February 1996, at the same time as the WRX V-Limited. All examples were painted Sports Blue.

Bodywork:
Rear emblem in white, stating Subaru were 1995 WRC Champions.

Interior:
Aluminium limited-edition plate with serial number. STI-style seats with STI logo and signatures of Colin McRae and Derek Ringer woven into upholstery.

Engine:
1994cc engine with 260bhp.

Running gear:
Standard suspension.

WRX STI Version III V-Limited (1997)

555 Saloons, 555 Sports Wagons
This was introduced in January 1997 and was promoted as a celebration of the 1996 World Rally Championship victory. They were based on the standard Version III cars, and all examples were finished in Sports Blue.

Bodywork:
Boot lid with roundel badge stating Subaru were 1996 WRC champions.
Limited-edition plate below roundel badge.
Roof vent.
Green-tinted glass.
Pink six-star grille logo.

Interior:
Aluminium limited-edition plate with serial number.
1996 WRC victory emblem woven into seat upholstery.

Engine:
1994cc engine with 260bhp.

Running gear:
Standard suspension.

WRX Type R STI Coupé (1997)

Unknown Total
The Type R STI Coupé was intended to reflect the intro-

duction of the two-door coupé body shell for the latest WRC cars, but its other attributes were those of the WRX STI Version III. The model was announced in January 1997 at the same time as the WRX STI Version III V-Limited, and was built to special order only. Only three colours were available: Chase Yellow, Feather White and Sonic Blue Mica.

Bodywork:
Body-colour front lip spoiler.
Body-colour side skirts.
Deep rear valance in body colour.
Body-colour door handles.
Power-fold door mirrors.
Body-colour mirror bodies.
Boot lid with Type R badge and 1996 WRC victory logo.
WRX decals ahead of rear wheels.
Rear side windows and rear screen with blackout tint.

Interior:
Automatic air conditioning.
Blue-faced instrument dials.
Seats in grey and black with red accents and 555 SWRT logo.
Electric windows.
Central locking.

Engine:
1994cc engine with 280bhp and 253lb ft.
Intercooler with automatic water-spray.

Running gear:
Close-ratio gearbox from Type RA.
DCCD.
Standard suspension.
Power-assisted steering.
Larger rear brake discs.
Five-spoke 7Jx16 wheels in gold (with Sonic Blue Mica) or black (with Chase Yellow and Feather White).

WRX Type RA STI Version IV V-Limited Saloon (1998); WRX Type R STI Version IV V-Limited Coupé (1998)

555 Examples; Unknown Total
The January 1998 V-Limited models were Version IV types and were used as a celebration of Subaru's 1997 WRC

victory. All models were based on the current Type RA and were finished in Sonic Blue Mica. Sales of the Type R models ended in March 1998.

Bodywork:
Body-colour side skirts.
Body-colour door handles.
Power-fold door mirrors.
Body-colour mirror bodies.
Six-star grille logo in cherry red.
Boot lid with 1997 WRC victory logo.

Interior:
Limited-edition plaque on centre console.
Automatic air conditioning.
Special logos on upholstery.
Red stitching on steering wheel and gear knob.
Electric windows.
Central locking.

Engine:
1994cc engine with 280bhp and 253lb ft.

Running gear:
Close-ratio gearbox from Type RA.
Helical front LSD.
Quick-ratio steering rack.
Standard suspension.
Five-spoke 7Jx16 wheels in gold.

WRX Type R V-Limited Coupé (1998)

1000 Examples
This was a third special edition introduced in January 1998 to celebrate Subaru's 1997 WRC victory. It was based on the two-door body shell.

Bodywork:
Roof vent.
Boot spoiler (lower than Type RA) with third brake light.
Fog lights.
Black six-star grille logo.
Power-fold door mirrors.
Body-colour mirror bodies.
Boot lid with 1997 WRC victory logo.

Interior:
Special seat trim and logos.
Black stitching on steering wheel and gear knob.
Limited-edition plaque on centre console.
Automatic air conditioning.
Electric windows.
Central locking.

Engine:
1994cc engine with 280bhp and 253lb ft.

Running gear:
Close-ratio gearbox from Type RA.
Standard suspension.
Five-spoke 7Jx16 wheels in gold.

22B (1998)

400 Examples
The 22B was an instant success when it was announced in Japan, and all 400 examples sold out extremely rapidly. For specification details, see the UK-market 22B listing (page [00]). There were differences in the lights, fuel filler neck, and speedometer, as well as a number of other minor changes. The Japanese cars did not have a rear fog light,

ABOVE AND OPPOSITE PAGE, TOP LEFT: *The 1998 22B was something very special, based on the two-door shell rather than the four-door and featuring a 2.2-litre engine and 'wide-body' modifications.*

and had a speed limiter on the engine, which restricted the maximum speed to 180km/h (112mph).

Three examples of the 22B had limited-edition number 000. Two went originally to Subaru's WRC drivers, Colin McRae and Nicky Grist. The third became a press car for Subaru in Japan. Car number 13 of the limited edition was never numbered, but went to the USA to become a demonstrator.

WRX STI Type RA Version V Limited Saloon (1998)

1000 Examples
The WRX STI Type RA Version V was announced in November 1998. All were finished in Sonic Blue Mica and had gold alloy wheels.

Bodywork:
Pink six-star grille logo.
Power-fold door mirrors.
Body-colour mirror bodies.
Body-colour door handles.

Interior:
Blue upholstery in front, with embroidered STI and Sub-aru logos.
Black rear upholstery.
Limited-edition plaque on centre console.
Automatic air conditioning.
Titanium gear knob.

Electric windows.
Central locking.

Engine:
1994cc engine with 280bhp and 253lb ft.

Running gear:
Helical front LSD.
Standard suspension.

WRX STI Type R Version V Limited Coupé (1998)

Unknown Total
This model was announced in November 1998 at the same time as the WRX Type RA Version V Limited and the WRX Type RA Limited. Production quantities are not known, but the car went out of production in March 1999 after just four months on sale. All were finished in Sonic Blue Mica and had gold alloy wheels.

Bodywork:
Pink six-star grille logo.
Roof vent.

Interior:
As standard.

Engine:
1994cc engine with 280bhp and 253lb ft.

Running gear:
Standard suspension.

WRX Type RA Limited (1998)

1000 Examples
This was one of the three WRX Limited models announced in November 1998. All models were finished in Sonic Blue Mica.

Bodywork:
Multi-reflector fog lights.
Rear spoiler with third brake light.
Power-fold door mirrors.

Body-colour mirror bodies.
Body-colour door handles.

Interior:
Blue front seats with embroidered STI and Subaru logos;
black rear seats.
Numbered limited-edition plate on centre console.
Automatic air conditioning.
Electric windows.
Central locking.

Engine:
1994cc engine with 280bhp and 253lb ft.

Running gear:
Standard suspension.
ABS standard.

WRX Type RA Limited Saloon (1999)

1000 Examples
This special edition was introduced in November 1999. All
examples were finished in Sonic Blue Mica.

Bodywork:
Black six-star grille badge.
Multi-reflector fog lights.
Lower rear spoiler.

Interior:
Blue front seat upholstery; black rear seat upholstery.
Blue dash insert panel.
Blue centre console with numbered limited-edition plate.
Aluminium pedals.
Automatic air conditioning.
Electric windows.
Central locking.

Engine:
1994cc engine with 280bhp and 253lb ft.

Running gear:
Standard suspension.
Gold-finish 16-inch six-spoke RAYS forged alloy wheels.
ABS standard.

WRX STI Type RA Version VI Limited Saloon (1999)

2000 Examples
This was another 2000 model-year special edition, intro-
duced in November 1999 and available only in Sonic Blue
Mica paint.

Bodywork:
Pink six-star grille badge.
Power-fold mirrors.
Body-colour mirror bodies.
Body-colour door handles.
Optional double-wing STI rear spoiler.

Interior:
Blue front seat upholstery with different logo from 1999-
model cars; black rear seat upholstery.
Blue dash insert panel.
Blue centre console with numbered limited-edition plate.
Aluminium pedals.
Titanium gear knob.
Automatic air conditioning.
Electric windows.
Central locking.

Engine:
1994cc engine.

Running gear:
Standard suspension.
Gold-finish 16-inch six-spoke RAYS forged alloy wheels.

WRX Type R STI Version VI Limited Coupé (1999)

1000 Examples
This 2000 model-year special edition was introduced in
November 1999 and came only in Sonic Blue Mica paint.

Bodywork:
Pink six-star grille badge.
Roof vent.

Interior:
Blue front seat upholstery with different logo from 1999-

model cars; black rear seat upholstery.
Blue dash insert panel.
Blue centre console with numbered limited-edition plate.
Aluminium pedals.
Titanium gear knob.

Engine:
1994cc engine.

Running gear:
Standard suspension.
Gold-finish 16-inch six-spoke RAYS forged alloy wheels.

WRX STI Version VI Limited Sports Wagon (1999)

500 Examples
This was the fourth special edition introduced in November 1999 for the Japanese domestic market. Like the others, it was available only in Sonic Blue Mica paint.

Bodywork:
Pink six-star grille badge.

Interior:
Standard seats; front pair have blue accents and embroidered SWRT and STI logos.
Blue dash insert panel.
Blue centre console with numbered limited-edition plate.
Aluminium pedals.
Titanium gear knob.
Kenwood ICE system with MD and CD.

Engine:
1994cc engine.

Running gear:
Standard suspension.
Gold-finish 16-inch six-spoke RAYS forged alloy wheels.

S201 STI (2000)

300 Examples
This was the first of the STI S-series limited editions. It was based on the Electra One concept vehicle revealed at the 1999 Tokyo Show and the 2000 Tokyo Auto Salon. The base vehicle was a four-door WRX STI saloon and the S201 was announced in April 2000.

Bodywork:
Arctic Silver Metallic paint with dark grey detailing.
Deep front spoiler with large air intake.
Large bonnet air scoop.
Side skirts and rear door spats.
Double-wing rear spoiler.
Centre rear stoplight in special boot-lid attachment.

Interior:
Blue front seats with embroidered STI logo.
Blue-painted dash insert and centre panel.
Numbered limited-edition plaque on centre console.
Aluminium pedals.
Titanium gear lever knob.

Engine:
1994cc engine with 305PS (300bhp) and 353Nm (260lb ft).
STI sports ECU.
Large-bore exhaust system.

Running gear:
Front LSD.
Height-adjustable suspension.
Rear links with 'pillow-ball' bushes.
Red-painted brake calipers.
Gold-finish 7J x 17 RS-Zero wheels.

AUSTRALIAN SPECIAL EDITIONS

WRX Rallye (1996)

120 Examples
This was a strictly cosmetic limited edition, based on the standard saloon but finished in the blue associated with the World Rally cars.

Bodywork:
As standard WRX.

Interior:
STi-style seats with special upholstery.

Engine:
1994cc engine with 260bhp.

Running gear:
Standard suspension.
Gold STi five-spoke wheels.

Club Spec (1997)

Unknown Total
The 1997 Club Spec limited edition was available as either a saloon or a Sports Wagon. It proved a big hit and, according to press releases, sold out within eight days.

Bodywork:
Blue Mica paint.
Special 'Club Spec' decals.

Interior:
Seats with red inserts.

Engine:
1994cc.

Running gear:
15-inch five-spoke wheels with gold finish.

Silver Anniversary

Unknown Total
This was a 1998-season limited edition available as either a saloon or a Sports Wagon. It was based on the WRX with automatic gearbox that was then available in Australia.

Bodywork:
Black Mica paint.

Interior:
Special seats with leather upholstery.
CD player.

Engine:
1994cc.

Running gear:
Automatic gearbox.
Gold-finish wheels.

WRX Club Spec Evo 2 (1998)

230 Examples
Introduced in May 1998, this car was more or less a repeat of the 1997 Club Spec limited edition, but incorporated the basic 1998 specification.

Bodywork:
Blue paint.
Special decals on front wings and rear doors.

Interior:
Suede trim on seats and door inserts.
Nardi steering wheel with red stitching.
Quickshift gear change.
Gear knob with leather knob and red stitching.
Tracker anti-theft system.

Engine:
1994cc engine.

Running gear:
Standard suspension.
16-inch five-spoke wheels with gold finish.

WRX Classic (1999)

150 Examples
Introduced in February 1999, this is said to have been a very successful Australian limited edition. An automatic-gearbox model was available.

Bodywork:
Black Mica, Dark Blue Mica or Green Mica paint.
Colour-coded door handles and mirrors.

Interior:
Beige leather upholstery.

Momo steering wheel with leather and wood rim.
Leather and wood gear knob, with chrome gate on manual cars.
Metallic-finish instrument panel.
Keyless entry system with alarm.
CD player.

Engine:
1994cc engine.

Running gear:
Five-speed manual or four-speed automatic gearbox.
Standard suspension.

WRX Club Spec Evo 3 (1999)

150 Examples
This was a 150-strong special edition announced in June 1999 and based on the standard WRX with five-speed manual gearbox.

Bodywork:
Blue Steel Mica paint.
Body-colour side skirts, door handles and mirrors.
Special badges.

Interior:
Blue alcantara upholstery.

Engine:
1994cc engine.

Running gear:
Standard suspension.

WRX Special Edition (1999)

Unknown Total
Introduced in December 1999, this was identical to the earlier WRX Classic from February 1999 (see above). It was produced because the earlier limited edition had proved so successful in the showrooms.

WRX Club Spec Evo 4 (2000)

300 Examples
This model was announced at the Adelaide Show in March 2000. It was available as either a saloon or a Sports Wagon.

Bodywork:
Yellow paint.
Colour-keyed door mirrors and door handles.
Black five-spoke alloys.
Black sill extensions.
Evo 4 decals on rear doors and boot lid.

Interior:
Yellow trim inserts (on saloon models).
Momo steering wheel with airbag.
Upgraded ICE system with CD player.
STI-style metal-finish dash panel.
Numbered limited-edition plaque on centre console.

Engine:
1994cc engine.

Running gear:
Standard suspension.

CHAPTER 6

THE SECOND GENERATION

Sometimes, an old cliché is the only way to describe a certain situation, and there was no doubt that the first-generation Impreza was a hard act to follow. But for the GD models that were announced in the autumn of 2000 as 2001 model-year cars, the company had played it safe. The new cars drew on all the strengths of the old ones – even looked a lot like them – but also addressed a number of the shortcomings that had become apparent since the originals had been introduced eight years earlier.

The most important change lay in the structure, which was made considerably stiffer than before. There were good reasons for this: the additional strength in the body shell enabled the car to meet known and anticipated crash-resistance legislation in world markets, while also improving on-the-limit handling. The fact that it made the car even better equipped to take the punishment of a typical WRC event was a bonus that was certainly not overlooked during the development stage.

Various different figures for the additional stiffness of the body shell have been quoted over the years, and authorities have given figures varying between 120 per cent and 250 per cent improvement over the last of the GC cars. Subaru themselves actually claimed that the GD saloon shell was 148 per cent stiffer torsionally and 82 per cent stiffer in beam rigidity; the estate was slightly less stiff, because it had no rear bulkhead. Much of the additional strength came from what was effectively a ring of steel around the body at the B-pillar. The pillars themselves had no fewer than eight layers of high-strength, high-tensile steel with a round steel bar running through the middle. Some sources have claimed that this steel bar caused some difficulties in the early days for rescue workers who were trying to cut through the B-pillars after an accident.

Inevitably, this additional strength brought with it additional weight. When the British magazine *Autocar* reviewed one of the new WRX models in its issue dated 25 October 2000, it recorded a weight increase of 150kg (330lb). Such a significant addition could only reduce the Impreza's agility, and this indeed proved to be the case. However, it also had a beneficial effect on refinement, making a contribution to ride comfort and even to noise levels inside the car.

As before, the new body shell was made available as a four-door saloon and an estate, but this time there was no two-door coupé. The overall lines of the car were readily identifiable, and in that sense the design was rather conservative. Most of the expected styling cues were there, too, with the bonnet-mounted air scoop, the twin exhausts and the huge round driving lights in the front apron.

On top of that, body designer Mamoru Ishii also introduced some quite radical changes. On the turbocharged saloons (but not the smaller-engined cars or any of the estates), perhaps the most obvious additions were the flared wings, and all models had large round headlamps that incorporated the turn indicators. It was this new front end, which gave the car a rather sad expression, that provoked the strongest reactions. Even before the car reached the showrooms, there were indications that the new styling had not been welcomed in all quarters. Ford had made a similar mistake with the front-end styling of the MkII Scorpio in 1994, and it is surprising that Subaru had not learned from that.

When *Autocar* published impressions of an early Japanese production car in its issue of 20 September 2000, the new front-end design was already 'controversial'. According to the magazine's Japanese correspondent, 'rumours [were] already afoot that a European styling consultant

The second-generation Impreza was readily recognizable as a relative of the first, but the new front end was immediately controversial. The problem was those big round headlights. This is a 2001-model WRX for the UK market.

LEFT AND BELOW: *The second-generation cabin was still drably grey, although there had been some attempt to give it highlights in the upholstery pattern and with silver notes around the heater control panel and air vents. A four-spoke Momo steering wheel helped, too.*

GD Models, 2000–2007

Engine (2.0-litre)
Subaru EJ20 horizontally opposed four-cylinder. Aluminium block and heads; turbocharger with air-cooled intercooler; various different types of turbocharger were used for different variants.

Capacity	1994cc
Bore and stroke	92 x 75mm
Compression ratio	Varies for different types and models
Fuel system	Multi-point injection
Valve gear	Four overhead camshafts (two on each cylinder bank); four valves per cylinder

Japanese-spec engines in manual-gearbox saloons:
250PS at 6000rpm and 245lb ft at 3600rpm
(2001 models)

Japanese-spec STI engines:
280PS at 6400rpm and 274lb ft at 4400rpm

US-spec engines:
230PS at 6000rpm and 217lb ft at 4000rpm

UK-spec engines:
218PS at 5600rpm and 215lb ft at 3600rpm
(2001 models)
222PS at 5600rpm and 221lb ft at 4000rpm
(2002–2005 models)
265PS at 6000rpm and 253lb ft at 4000rpm (STI models)

Engine (2.5-litre; export markets, 2006–2007)
Subaru EJ25 horizontally opposed four-cylinder. Aluminium block and heads; turbocharger with air-cooled intercooler; various different types of turbocharger were used for different variants.

Capacity	2457cc
Bore and stroke	99.5 x 79mm
Compression ratio	Varies for different types and models
Fuel system	Multi-point injection
Valve gear	Four overhead camshafts (two on each cylinder bank); four valves per cylinder; ACVS (Active Valve Control System)

UK-spec engines:
230PS at 5600rpm and 236lb ft at 3600rpm
(WRX models)

276PS at 6000rpm and 289lb ft at 4000rpm
(WRX STI models)

Transmission
Permanent four-wheel drive with viscous-coupled centre differential and limited-slip rear differential; VTD standard with automatic gearbox; DCCD on WRX STI models.

Gearbox
Five-speed manual with overdrive fourth and fifth gears (WRX models)
Six-speed manual with overdrive fifth and sixth gears (WRX STI models)
Automatic available in some countries

Final drive gearing
4.11:1 with five-speed gearbox.
3.90:1 with six-speed gearbox.

Steering
Power-assisted rack and pinion, speed-sensitive, with anti-kickback damper valve.

Suspension
Front: MacPherson struts with coil springs, forged aluminium lower arms, L-shaped transverse link strut, and anti-roll bar.
Rear: MacPherson struts with coil springs, dual links, trailing arms and anti-roll bar.

Brakes
Servo-assisted diagonally split dual-circuit hydraulic system with pressure limiting valve; four-channel, four-sensor ABS with electronic brakeforce distribution
Ventilated front discs with four-piston calipers (some models with six-piston calipers); ventilated rear discs with two-piston calipers.

Weights and measures
Wheelbase	2525mm (99.5in)
Front track	1485mm (58.5in)
Rear track	1480mm (58.25in)
Length	4465mm (175.75in)
Width	1740mm (68.5in)
Height	1440mm (56.75in)
Wheels	17in alloy, later 18in
Tyres	Various sizes (see text)
Unladen weight	1385kg–1470kg (3053lb–3240lb), depending on model

may be called on for a hasty restyling job of certain details before the car reaches British dealers'. It was all too much for some buyers. 'We're already hearing reports of customers cancelling orders because they can't get on with the shape,' claimed the same magazine's issue of 25 October, just a week after the new car had been displayed in Britain for the first time at the 2000 British International Motor Show held in Birmingham's NEC.

There were also a number of modifications that affected the chassis components, too. The front suspension was now mounted on a sub-frame, which made its own contribution to overall rigidity. The spring and damper ratings were changed, and the steering was tightened up with more rigid rack mountings and a modified UJ within that rack. Like the latest Legacy, it felt lighter. The tracks on the hot Impreza saloons (but not the estates) were 20mm (0.8in) wider. On the WRX cars, there were now 17-inch wheels with 7.5J rims and wider 215/45ZR17 tyres. To a degree, these changes had been forced on the designers by the additional weight of the car, and by the fact that this now moved the Impreza's roll centre some 33mm (1.3in) higher up.

One of the most common criticisms of the first-generation cars had been that their interiors lacked sparkle. As a result, for the GD series cars, the cabin was reworked. Criticisms of minimal headroom in the rear were also addressed. The cabin was in fact 21mm (0.85in) wider, and the 30mm (1.2in) of extra headroom now made occupancy of the rear seat much more comfortable for tall passengers. However, the makeover of the rest of the cabin had not really gone far enough. Height-adjustable front seats were a welcome addition, and there was a choice between 'sports' front seats or rally-style buckets, the latter without the side airbags that were standard with the sports-seat option. The driving position remained excellent, with a steering wheel adjustable for rake, clear instruments and a good view all around the car. Unfortunately, the overall ambience was again dominated by sensible but boring plain grey plastic. There was going to be plenty for the Impreza aftermarket to tackle.

That same aftermarket was also going to have plenty to work on under the bonnet, at least as far as the WRX was concerned. Its engine was still the all-alloy 2.0-litre 'boxer' four, unchanged in essentials from that of the final GC-series cars. There were some improvements, though: a new catalytic converter in the exhaust, a larger Mitsubishi TD04L turbocharger and modified wastegate, and an intercooler that was 11 per cent larger than before were all fac-

tors in bringing the torque peak lower down the rev range (to 3600rpm from 4000rpm). With 80 per cent of maximum torque available below 2200rpm, the engine was now much more responsive, providing the improved driveability that had been a key aim for the Japanese engineers. On UK-specification cars, maximum power was still 215PS even though the Japanese-specification cars had a lot more. Maximum torque was just 1lb ft greater than before, and even though this was generated at lower engine speeds, the figure did sound suspiciously like a token gesture.

There was of course the usual array of engine options for the everyday saloons and estates, but at the top end of the range Subaru had decided to simplify matters. Very welcome in the UK was the fact that the 'Impreza 2000 Turbo AWD' name had now been dropped, and the top-end cars were now known as Impreza WRX models. At launch, their prices were £21,495 for the saloon and £21,995 for the estate, maintaining the traditional £500 difference between the two.

UK MODELS FOR 2001

The UK-spec cars went on sale in November 2000, and were drawn from the middle of the 2.0-litre range as it was presented in Japan. At the bottom of that was a naturally-aspirated car with 153bhp, and at the top was the model now badged as an STI, boasting over 280bhp. The UK cars were pitched between these extremes, and came with 218bhp turbocharged engines. These had lost nearly 30bhp as compared to their 247bhp Japanese WRX equivalents, thanks to the need to meet European regulations relating to noise and exhaust emissions. In Subaru's nomenclature, these were Revision A cars.

It was *Autocar* who published the first full road-test in the UK, and its review dated 25 October 2000 concluded that the Impreza WRX 'remains the definitive affordable performance saloon for the enthusiast'. There were a few negatives, though: the testers felt that a certain amount of performance had been traded for refinement, and the 5.7-second 0–60mph time suggested that the new car was slower than the one it replaced. Fuel consumption was again not the Impreza's strong suit, with an overall of 15.1 l/100km (18.7mpg) – the same disappointing figure as the old car achieved.

Yet most of the old characteristics were still present. 'Steering is quite brilliant,' said *Autocar*, 'although it takes some time to get used to it.... delicacy and accuracy are

its two best traits.' The brakes were still excellent, and 'traction out of any bend is superb. But put the power down in mid-corner and the car just tightens its line and scoots off looking for the next bend. Back off in the same situation and the line tightens immediately.' Overall, the car was now much more useable: 'Subaru seems to have taken the concept of comfort to heart, because in a stroke it has turned the Impreza from being something to avoid over long distances into a comfortable saloon. New spring and damper ratings all round have given the suspension a compliance totally at odds with its ability to keep body movements under check at ridiculously high speeds. No matter what the surface, the car just copes.'

What Car? magazine also tested a WRX in its January 2001 issue and its verdict was that the car was a 'great update of [a] cult classic', but that it '[lacked] raw edge'. There was still a 'wonderful burble from the flat-four engine', and the magazine accurately nailed much of the Impreza's appeal by pointing out that it was 'one of those rare cars that flatters an average driver and delights a good one'. It was quicker than the old car to 60mph by half a second, although the higher overall gearing made it slower accelerating in the gears and made it feel less urgent as a whole. It was also 'all too easy to find yourself dawdling out of the power band' and then there seemed to be 'an age to wait before the engine [woke] up above 3000rpm'.

That said, the handling was sharper than before even though the steering had lost something, and the brakes were superb: 'Even on a damp test track, the stopping distances were up to the best we've seen. On the road...the pedal gives plenty of feel and a strong, progressive stop.'

Yet there was no doubt that sales of the hot Imprezas did slow down for a time, and that the new front-end styling seems to have been the major reason for this. With rival cars snapping at the WRX's heels – most notably the Mitsubishi Evo which, like the WRX, was based on a rally car – Subaru was not in a position to take chances. So during 2001, the company embarked on an urgent facelift programme for the whole Impreza range. As much face-saver as facelift, this was announced for the 2003 model-year cars after the GD-series 'bug-eye' models had been on sale for only two years.

Just one special-edition Impreza WRX was made available during the lifetime of the 'bug-eye' second-generation models: the UK300. It was prepared by Prodrive with the approval of Subaru UK and carried the standard factory warranty, becoming available towards the end of May 2001. There are further details of this 300-strong special edition in Chapter 8, but it is worth noting here that the car was prepared with input from Peter Stevens, the styling consultant who had also worked on the WRC cars and had overseen the Prodrive P1.

THE 2002 MODEL-YEAR: ENTER THE STI

For the 2002 model-year, Subaru UK took note of the criticisms that had been levelled at the 2001 models. So the Revision B models for UK buyers had different gear ratios, this time the same as those of the models for the Japanese domestic market. Their aim was to improve

acceleration and to counter claims that the new cars were slower than the old models. Meanwhile, the parent company's engineers and designers raced to change the disappointing 'face' that had been introduced on the 2001-model cars (and, as it turned out, to upgrade the car in other respects). What no one knew at the time – although many may have suspected it – was that the facelift was being carried out by a British design consultant.

More importantly for the moment, perhaps, the 2002 model-year brought the UK market its first official imports of STI models (the 22B limited edition excepted) and, as had always been the case in Japan, these offered even higher performance than could be had from the WRX cars. The combined effect of quicker WRX models and ultra-quick STI types ensured that there was no need for any high-performance limited editions in the UK during the 2002 model-year.

The WRX STI was introduced Europe-wide at the Frankfurt Show in September 2001, and UK sales began in January 2002. It represented a new flagship for the Impreza range, and was understandably more expensive than the standard WRX, with a showroom price of £25,995. The headline news was a higher state of engine tune, and the WRX STI now had 261bhp at 6000rpm with 253lb ft of torque at 4000rpm. To keep things cool under the bonnet when the car was driven hard, the intercooler was now fitted with a water-spray, which was activated automatically at a pre-set rev limit. A warning light on the rev counter inside the car told the driver when this was happening. The exhaust was a big-bore type with a single tailpipe.

On top of that, the WRX STI had the STI-developed six-speed gearbox with both fifth and sixth as overdrive gears, plus Suretrac limited-slip differentials both front and rear. Inverted dampers and a faster steering rack were matched by big-diameter Brembo brakes, and there were Bridgestone RE040 225/45ZR17 tyres on gold-painted five-spoke 7.5J wheels. Inside the car, the trim featured blue alcantara with black seat bolsters, STI logos on the seats, and red stitching on the leather covers for steering wheel, gear knob and handbrake grip. The instrument binnacle now had the rev counter in the centre, making it the largest and most prominent of the three dials.

From the outside, there were of course additional recognition features. Gold-painted wheels aside, the WRX STI was distinguished by its smoked-glass projector-beam headlights and larger air intake. It could be had in just four colours: WR Blue Mica, Blue-Black Mica, Premium Silver Mica and Pure White. Underneath, at least on the UK-market cars, the new models also had improved rust-proofing.

There was even better to be had, at a price. Prodrive produced its own edition of the WRX STI for £27,495. There were 750 cars, available only in WR Blue Mica or Blue-Black Mica, but featuring a deeper front bumper, special grille and distinctive front and rear spoilers. Inside, the cars also had blue-faced instruments with red needles. The WRX STI certainly did the trick for Subaru in the UK. By the autumn of 2002, the company was claiming that the model had accounted for 30 per cent of Impreza sales over the nine months since it had gone on sale. It left no one in any doubt that more performance sold more cars.

THE 2003 MODELS: A NEW FACE

The results of the facelift were revealed to European buyers at the Paris Motor Show in September 2002, and the revised cars reached UK showrooms in February 2003. Although the cosmetic improvements attracted most attention, and no doubt persuaded many buyers back into the Subaru showrooms, in fact the revised cars also incorporated a number of engineering improvements. Most of these – at least, according to Subaru press announcements – were designed to keep the works rally cars competitive for the 2003 WRC season.

The major cosmetic changes were to that controversial front end, which took on a more aggressive appearance, with elongated headlamps that recalled those of the first-generation Impreza. Enthusiasts soon took to calling these 'crocodile eyes'. Lamps, wings, bonnet and bumper had in fact all been redesigned; the bonnet was now more steeply raked (partly to improve pedestrian safety in an accident) and incorporated an even bigger air scoop than before. At the rear, there were more subtle changes to the bumper and light units. The flanks, however, remained the same, and, as before, the Sports Wagon estates lacked the wide wings of the saloons and also had narrower front and rear tracks.

Still working on the interior, Subaru had introduced new cloth for the upholstery and a new centre console that joined the centre 'stack' to the gearshift surround. On the WRX models, the rev counter was now located in the middle of the instrument binnacle, as on the WRX STI models, and all three dials took on silver frames. The front seats now had active head restraints, the brake pedal was designed to snap off under impact to protect the driver's leg and foot in a collision, and there were ISO-FIX child seat restraints in the rear to ensure that the car remained viable as a family saloon. It all added up to a small improvement, but the cabin was still desperately bland and not at all worthy of a performance car. A dual-stage passenger's airbag, standard side airbags and deadlocks with anti-theft shields were other worthwhile touches.

The redesign of both interior and exterior had been carried out by Peter Stevens, who had already worked on the WRC rally cars for Prodrive. As his website –peter-stevens.co.uk – makes clear, the project had been initiated in 2001 and had taken 13 months. Stevens had been responsible for design direction, modelling and prototype build, and the result was improved sales performance – precisely what Subaru wanted.

Subaru had a facelift designed in double-quick time. The new 'face' for 2003 – actually seen on a 2004 car – offered much more stylish headlights.

Interior changes were part of the new look, too. The rev counter had moved to the centre of the instrument cluster and the speedometer was off to the right; the change had occurred for 2002 on STI models, and followed on the WRX a year later.

Reasoning that they were in danger of losing their market to rivals – exemplified by the new generation of hot hatches such as the Ford Focus RS, Honda Civic Type-R, and Volkswagen Golf R32 – Subaru had also taken action to restore customer interest in other areas. A key factor was a drop in the showroom price, so that the WRX saloon now cost a shade under £20,000 while the estate cost £20,495. But there had also been an improvement in performance. A remapped ECU and sodium-filled valves were the main changes, although the new engines also demanded 97-octane unleaded fuel if they were to give of their best. Power was now 222bhp at 5600rpm, while torque had been increased to 221lb ft at 4000rpm, the latter slightly further up the rev range than before. The revised engine also put out lower levels of noxious emissions than before.

When *Autocar* sampled one of the new Imprezas for its issue of 29 January 2003, it chose the practical WRX Sports Wagon estate rather than the enthusiasts' favourite saloon. Recording 0–60mph in 5.5 seconds, the magazine commented on this 'slight but significant improvement in performance' with the revised engine. Response under 3000rpm was still poor, but the overall fuel average of 12.3 l/100km (23mpg) was a vast improvement on Imprezas the magazine had previously tested. The new model was 'still a seriously quick car and more than capable of holding its own against the new generation of super hatches'. *Autocar*'s verdict was a favourable one: 'As

an all-year, all-weather car, the kind that can thrill when asked, yet be content to cosset when the need arises, the Subaru has few peers at this price.'

The facelifted 2003 cars still came as WRX and WRX STI models, of course, the latter priced at £24,995. For those prepared to pay for even more performance, Prodrive was ready and willing to oblige. On the standard WRX, the Prodrive Performance Package lifted power to 265bhp, while on the WRX STI the equivalent package took power up to an astonishing 300bhp – all still from the basic Subaru turbocharged 2.0-litre flat-four.

Car magazine took a WRX STI with the 300bhp PPP to Kielder Forest to see how it performed on tracks that had once been used for the Rally of Great Britain. That it would perform well as a rally car in the right hands had never been in doubt, of course; the point of the exercise was more to get some exciting action photographs. In its March 2003 issue, the magazine was in no doubt about the STI variant's aggressively flamboyant looks. It was 'a little bit more mental, just that bit more angry' than the Imprezas that had gone before. 'It might be a bit hard for some,' they added, 'but you wouldn't buy one unless you were confident that it had the punch to back up the mouth.'

It undoubtedly did. It was also noisy on the long motorway run north, with a loud exhaust and a thrumming noise from the big rear wing spoiler. The air scoop on the bonnet wobbled, too. Before they had even reached Kielder

Forest, they had concluded that the car was hard work to drive: 'You'll get out of this car shaking with adrenalin. And absolutely knackered.' The car had 'lots of technology but precious little finesse, bags of personality but very little civility'. There was, at least, no question that the Impreza – in this version at least – had retained its hard edge of old.

2004 AND 2005: CONSOLIDATION

The 2003-season changes were enough to keep UK Impreza sales buoyant for both the 2003 and 2004 seasons, and the Subaru team's sterling performance in the World Rally Championship played its own important part in keeping interest in the WRX and WRX STI alive. Petter Solberg's WRC win prompted the production of a 1000-strong world-wide special edition which reached the UK in January 2004 complete with additional Prodrive modifications. It is an indication of the UK market's importance to WRX and WRX STI sales that exactly half of those 1000 cars were earmarked for the UK. Full details of the WR1 edition, as the UK knew it, are given in Chapter 8.

The next major changes for UK-spec cars were made for the 2005 model-year, and closely paralleled those that were made for Japanese domestic models at the same time. The WRX now took on the inverted damper struts that had been introduced on the WRX STI, and also gained revised steering geometry. There was a greater use of aluminium suspension components to reduce unsprung weight and so improve the ride and handling, and the

brake calipers were painted red to suit a fashion for making these components stand out behind multi-spoked alloy wheels. Other tweaks to the braking system improved its feel. Inside the car, the cabin revisions included a new three-spoke steering wheel, modified switches and controls, a new centre console and a generally more luxurious feel to the trim. The instrument dials now had red markings on a black background.

The WRX STI of course went several steps further. In Japan, more engine torque was gained from modifications to the intercooler and the exhaust system, resulting in 303lb ft at 4400rpm, although these changes did not filter through to the UK. Limited-slip differentials were once again standard at both ends of the car, the front one having an improved helical design. Also standard was a bias control for the centre differential, which enabled the driver to adjust the power delivery between front and rear wheels. Although it was of precious little use outside a rally special stage, this new Driver Controlled Centre Differential (DCCD) certainly appealed to buyers with a taste for gadgetry – and for those who knew what they were doing, it could be adjusted to improve turn-in to corners or straight-line stability. It incorporated an automatic setting, which adjusted the bias without driver intervention by using inputs from a yaw rate sensor. Also inspired by the rally cars, and again of little use in everyday driving, was an undertray, which smoothed out the airflow below the engine and floor pan.

Down below, modifications brought changes in some of the major dimensions, as the rear track went up by 10mm

Red-painted brake calipers show through the wheels on a 2005 UK-market WRX.

The red-painted calipers are also visible on a 2005 WRX Sports Wagon. The facelift of 2003 certainly helped the car's looks, but the five-door Impreza was always a rather ungainly beast.

World Rally blue and gold-painted brake calipers behind gold 10-spoke wheels distinguish this WRX STI Type-UK model for 2005 – the first STI type officially imported into the UK. Note the STI logo on the cover over the driving-lamp apertures, the special decal on the front door and, of course, the tall rear wing spoiler.

Under the bonnet, the special STI treatment continued. Note the red-painted inlet manifold and the STI logo on the intercooler.

ABOVE AND BELOW: *The STI interior was much more attractive than that of the standard WRX type, with blue upholstery sections, three-spoke wheel, pink STI logos and stitching, and a redesigned centre console.*

(0.4in) and the wheelbase increased by 15mm (0.6mm). Essentially, there had been some changes to the suspension geometry as well as to the spring and damper rates. Bigger anti-roll bars accompanied a modified steering rack; there were stronger front strut mounts and stronger front hubs and bearings; and the rear suspension links were now made completely of aluminium alloy. The tyres were now 235/45ZR17s on 8J ten-spoke alloy wheels, and for effect the brake calipers were painted gold. There were minor modifications to the rear wings to accommodate these new wider tyres.

To complete the picture, the WRX STI had its own special steering wheel, which was a version of the latest three-spoke type in the WRX, but bearing an STI logo in the centre instead of the six stars of Subaru. The black cloth on the seat bolsters was made of a different, rougher material, which was claimed to help keep occupants in place during hard cornering. The cars were also fitted with an immobilizer – with such a desirable specification, this was more or less a necessity to prevent insurance premiums going through the roof.

From May 2005, there were yet more temptations in UK showrooms. For a period of three months, Subaru UK offered a free Prodrive power upgrade to all buyers of a WRX or WRX STI. It was of course optional, because not every buyer wanted to take on the higher insurance premiums that came with power of 256bhp on a WRX and 300bhp on a WRX STI, but it certainly proved popular. Then there was also a limited edition of 300 WRX 300 cars, of which there are more details in Chapter 8.

2006: UP TO 2.5 LITRES

The 2006 models introduced in autumn 2005 underwent two major changes, as they took on a new-style front end that is commonly described as the 'hawk-eye' type, and switched from the 2.0-litre turbocharged engine to a 2.5-litre turbocharged engine. These models were known to Subaru as the Revision F types, while enthusiasts sometimes call them the GD/F models

The new front-end design was intended to bring the Impreza into line with other models in the Subaru family. It consisted of a three-section mesh grille, which was said to resemble a jet intake and wings, and so to pay homage to the origins of Subaru in the Nakajima Aircraft Company. (Nakajima had never put a jet aircraft into production, but that fact was conveniently ignored for publicity purposes!) The new style had been previewed at the 2003 Tokyo Show on the R2 concept car, and had first appeared in production in January 2005, on the Subaru R1 'kei' car ('kei' cars are very small models designed to meet Japanese city-car size regulations). The Impreza also sported new headlight units to suit, with smoke-tinted lenses, as well as new bumpers and tail-lights.

The new three-element grille design had been previewed on the R2 concept car, shown at Tokyo in 2003.

There was new definition in the tail-lights for 2006, with projector-like sections in the lower segment.

Facelift time again: the three-section grille introduced on 2006 models was intended to bring them into line with the new Subaru family look.

Also new for 2006 was a larger 2.5-litre edition of the 'boxer' engine. The overall under-bonnet layout was much as before, though.

The new engine had meanwhile come about because European regulations relating to exhaust emissions were scheduled to become stricter from January 2006, and it was easier to meet these with the 2.5-litre engine than by further modification of the older 2.0-litre. The engine was in fact not totally new. It was a derivative of the familiar 'boxer' four-cylinder, with a bigger bore and a longer stroke, and had been available for the best part of a decade in naturally aspirated form in some Subaru models for Australia and North America.

In turbocharged form for the WRX and WRX STI models, the 2.5-litre engine incorporated a variable valve timing system that Subaru knew as AVCS (Active Valve Control System), and an Electronic Throttle Control System. The pistons were cas- aluminium types with a lower rate of thermal expansion than the forged types in the 2.0-litre engine, and there were new engine mountings made of liquid-filled plastic to reduce vibration transmission; these were also seen on the 2.0-litre engine for the Japanese domestic market, and gave some trouble in service. With

227bhp (230PS) and 236lb ft (320Nm), the 2.5-litre engine offered useful increases over the older 2.0-litre type, but it was clear that it had not been stretched very far for this initial Impreza application.

As before, the two models of interest to enthusiasts were the WRX and WRX STI. The WRX retained its bargain-basement pricing; for 2006 it cost £20,900. It had silver 17-inch wheels through which its red brake calipers were visible. There were body-colour sill panels, the usual aluminium bonnet, and a limited-slip rear differential. Inside, there were sporty-looking drilled aluminium pedals, and the ICE system now had four speakers, although its sound quality was still poor by the standards of the day. The WRX came in five colours: Bright Red, Crystal Grey Metallic, Obsidian Black Pearl, Premium Silver Metallic and Pure White.

The WRX STI cost considerably more, at £26,995. It had the new 2.5-litre engine in a much higher state of tune, with 276bhp at 6000rpm and 289lb ft at 4000pm. With a taller final drive and six-speed gearbox, it was also

The WRX STI Type-UK for 2006 was a street racer's delight, with a huge single-exit exhaust for optimum sound effects, and a tall wing spoiler. The boot-lid badging on this 2006 car has the pink STI logo and pink 'Type UK' plate badge.

For 2006, an extra-cost SL pack was available in the UK; the leather seats show that this car has it.

considerably faster, reaching 60mph from rest in 5 seconds dead and going on to a top speed of 254km/h
(158mph). There was no mistaking the car from a distance,
as it sported a taller rear wing spoiler than the WRX, plus
a roof spoiler just above the rear window.

Equipment levels were higher, too. In addition to limited-slip differentials front and rear, it had the DCCD. There
were Brembo brakes, an undertray, and gold-painted 8Jx17
wheels, and the interior boasted blue alcantara upholstery
with an STI logo on the front bucket seats, red stitching
on the leather steering wheel, gear knob and handbrake
covers, and an aluminium gear lever surround. The rev
counter had an adjustable warning indicator to prevent
over-revving, too. Less visibly, the WRX STI came with a
space-saver spare wheel and tyre, and an anti-theft tracking system to keep insurance premiums down. There were
four colour choices (Crystal Grey Metallic, Obsidian Black
Pearl, Premium Silver Metallic and WR Blue Mica), but
Pure White could also be had to special order.

It was very noticeable, at least on the UK cars for 2006,
that Subaru were aiming further up-market with the
WRX. The SL pack and the season's only special edition
(the Spec D) both made a preliminary stab in the direction of premium performance cars such as those from
BMW. The SL pack added leather upholstery, front-seat
heaters and a sunroof for an extra £1500.

The Spec D went a long stride further than the SL. It was
designed to appeal to a different set of buyers from those
who loved the aggressive, be-winged style of the WRX
STI and were content with its Spartan interior. The 'D' of the
designation stood for 'discreet', and this model was a WRX
STI that had been toned down to provide the performance
qualities in tandem with a greater degree of sophistication.
Subaru UK said it was intended for more mature buyers.
At £28,495 in March 2006, it was £1500 more than a standard WRX STI, and was thus the most expensive factory-
approved derivative then available in the UK. There are
more details of its specification in Chapter 8.

The SL pack was available on the five-door cars as well; the glass sunroof was part of the extra equipment.

UK Registrations

As with the first-generation cars, many Impreza Turbos owned by enthusiasts in the UK acquired special registration numbers. The majority did not, however, and it is therefore possible to tell from their number-plates the approximate date of first registration and therefore when they were new. The table below shows the periods when certain registration letters were current, and relates them to the Subaru model-year. Note that the relationship between registration period and model-year is not exact; it is possible that cars new at the end of a registration period may have acquired numbers relating to the following period.

Prefix letter	Registration period	Model-year
X	September 2000–February 2001	2001
Y	March 2001-August 2001	2001

Age identifier	Registration period	Model-year
51	September 2001–February 2002	2002
02	March 2002–August 2002	2002
52	September 2002–February 2003	2003
03	March 2003–August 2003	2003
53	September 2003–February 2004	2004
04	March 2004–August 2004	2004
54	September 2004–February 2005	2005
05	March 2005–August 2005	2005
55	September 2005–February 2006	2006
06	March 2006–August 2006	2006
56	September 2006–February 2007	2007
07	March 2007–August 2007	2007

SWAN-SONG: THE 2007 MODELS

The 2007-model Imprezas were to be the last of the GD-series cars, and yet development had not stood still. The body shell had been stiffened with additional bracing on the sides of the front bulkhead, and suspension changes had shortened the wheelbase very slightly, to 2515mm (99.4in). Specifically, the suspension control arms had reverted to an earlier design, which had also altered the castor angle, and the rear anti-roll bar had gone from 20mm (0.8in) to 19mm (0.75in) in diameter.

Under the bonnet, the 2.5-litre engine had now gone back to hard rubber engine mounts, as there had been so much trouble with the liquid-filled plastic types introduced for 2006. The injectors were changed and now had their feed pipes at the top rather than at the side, while cylinder heads had been redesigned with improved cooling, and the sodium-filled exhaust valves were deleted. Taller ratios for second, third and fourth gears improved both fuel economy and driveability, and the clutch-type rear limited-slip differential had given way to a torsen type.

Inside the car, the rear armrest had been modified to allow loads to be passed through from the boot, and on the dashboard the ashtray was replaced by a multi-purpose audio jack. Even though the ICE system was still not particularly good, at least owners could now plug in their MP3 player if they wished.

THE IMPREZA WRX GD WORLDWIDE

With the second-generation Impreza WRX, Subaru made the car available for the first time in the USA. So there were now four major specification groups: Asia-Pacific (which included the Japanese domestic market), Oceania (which included Australia), Europe (which included the UK), and North America (which primarily meant the USA).

Japanese-Spec Cars

2001 Model-Year (Revision A)
The 2001 models introduced to Japan in August 2000 included the WRX NB saloon with 250PS at 6000rpm and 333Nm at 3600rpm. The gearbox had close-ratio gears, which were unique to Japan at the time. These cars

had 16-inch wheels, with ventilated front and solid rear brake discs; there were twin-piston calipers at the front and single-piston types at the rear. There was a torsen limited-slip differential in the rear axle with a 4.44:1 final drive.

Throughout the production life of the GD cars, there was a stripped-out Japanese-market homologation special that was revised every year to keep the Group N and PWRC rally cars competitive. For 2001, this was the WRX Type RA STI. STI fog-light covers had white STI logos. This was the last season for the STI estate, which had an engine with only 271bhp (275PS).

2002 Model-Year (Revision B)
The 2002 models for Japan were announced in September 2001. The WRX NB saloon was essentially unchanged from the 2001 model, but it was heavier.

The WRX Type RA STI was replaced by the WRX STI Spec C, with lower weight from lighter glass and body panels. The 'C' stood for 'Competition', although it was rather confusing to make this name change at the same time as the change to Revision B models! New suspension control arms were used, to permit an increase in caster to 5 degrees from the original 3.5 degrees, and a consequent improvement in turn-in. This resulted in a wheelbase that was 15mm (0.6in) longer than before. The Spec C car also had a 13:1 steering rack ratio and a transmission oil cooler.

2003 Model-Year (Revision C)
The 2003 models were announced in November 2002, and now included a WRX NB-R model. Engine outputs were unchanged from those of 2002 models, but there were now 17-inch wheels. The brakes now had four-piston front calipers and two-piston rears, with ventilated brake discs at the rear as well as the front. The rear wing now incorporated side sections to raise it above the boot lid.

The Group N motorsport homologation for 2003 was done with a WRX STI.

2004 Model-Year (Revision D)
The WRX STI was now available with a Driver Controlled Centre Differential, and was the car used for Group N homologation. There were two new models, the WRX STI Spec C Type RA and WRX STI V-Limited. The Type RA car had a carbon-fibre lip on the front spoiler and a carbon-fibre rear wing. The engine was re-tuned and the car had

BBS alloy wheels. The Limited featured four-way adjustable dampers tuned by SWRT's Group N driver, Toshihiro Arai.

2004 Calendar Year (Revision E)
A new model called the WRX WR-limited was added to the range. This had an STI chin spoiler and STI rear spoiler, plus gold-painted RAYS wheels. The gearshift knob was made of titanium and carried a WR logo.

2005 Calendar Year (Revision F)
For 2005, WRX models gained a viscous limited-slip differential at the rear. They had gold-painted 7Jx17 wheels and could be fitted optionally with the WRX STI-type spoiler.

There were three models available in the STI range, the WRX STI, WRX STI Spec C and WRX STI Spec C Type RA. All had the new 8-inch wheel rims and slightly flared rear wings.

2006 Model-Year
Cars for the Japanese domestic market did not change to the 2.5-litre engine, but retained the 2.0-litre type that was still used in the rally cars because the FIA regulations had a 2.0-litre capacity ceiling.

The WRX STI Spec C Type RA was introduced in November 2005 as a limited run of 350 cars. It was visually distinguished from the standard Spec C car by 8Jx17 Enkei alloy wheels, an STI V-lip front spoiler, and a 110-mm (4.4-in) diameter tailpipe. The suspension was also uprated with STI components: four-way adjustable inverted struts, 'pillow-ball' rear suspension bushes, special springs (finished in pink), special lateral rear suspension links and rear trailing links, and a 21mm (0.85in) rear anti-roll bar.

2007 Model-Year (Revision G)
The 2007-model WRX cars were unchanged mechanically from the 2006 Japanese cars.

Both the WRX STI and WRX STI Spec C models had some minor modifications. A type VF43 turbocharger replaced the earlier VF39, bringing a slightly larger wastegate port that gave better control of boost. The injectors were now top-feed types instead of the earlier side-feed type, with associated modifications to the inlet manifold and the Tumble Valve Generators (TVGs) used to control emissions during a cold start of the engine. The six-speed gearbox also had different ratios.

The North American-Specification Imprezas

North America took a long time to warm to the Impreza, and did not receive official imports of the first-generation models. A WRX Sports Wagon had been shipped to the USA in the first quarter of 1995 for journalists to try, and a naturally aspirated 2.5RX coupé did the rounds of car shows in 1998 to gauge reaction. However, Subaru was in no hurry; as always, the company wanted to do things properly. So it was not until late 2000 that Subaru of America announced their plans to bring in Impreza WRX models from early in 2001.

The first US cars were Version B types and reached showrooms in March 2001. They had the 2-litre EJ205 engine with a Mitsubishi TD04-13T turbocharger in place of the type used in other markets. The headline figures of 227bhp at 6000rpm and 217lb ft at 4000rpm were attained at higher crankshaft speeds than on other engines. There were both manual and automatic transmission options, in each case with a 3.9:1 final drive and a viscous-coupled limited-slip differential at the rear. Automatic models had a Variable Torque Distribution all-wheel-drive system instead of the viscous-coupled centre differential found on the manual cars. The normal torque distribution provided 45 per cent to the front wheels and 55 per cent to the rears, but the VTD used multiple sensors to monitor front and rear driveshaft speeds, throttle position and gear selection and to decide when to alter the distribution for maximum traction and optimum handling.

There were ventilated front brake discs and solid rears, and two-piston front calipers with single-piston types at the rear. The wheels were 6.5Jx16-inch cast alloy versions of those used on the NB-specification cars in Japan.

2002 Models (Revision B)
As far as Japan was concerned, the 2002 models that became available in mid-2001 were still Version B types. They had brake ducting to carry air from the front bumper intake to the wheel well and so help brake cooling, but these had been discontinued before the end of the model-year.

2003 Models (Revision C)
Both saloons and Sports Wagons were still available, both with slightly larger front discs than on 2002 models. A new Sonic Yellow colour option was added, although the plan was to limit this to approximately 1500 cars.

The 2003 models incorporated some revisions based on experience with the cars in the USA. There had been some transmission failures caused by over-enthusiastic drivers, and Subaru countered these in two ways. First, they added a valve that prevented brutal standing starts; second, they fitted the 1mm (0.04in) wider gears from the Japanese-specification RA models to strengthen the gearbox itself. There had also been fuel leak problems at freezing temperatures, and so a shorter metal fuel pipe and longer connector hose were fitted in the vulnerable area under the inlet manifold.

Prices increased slightly for 2003, by $200, and a number of performance items were made available at extra cost. Also available at extra cost were 17-inch wheels.

2004 Models (Revision D)

The timing of new-model announcements needed in the USA combined with the shipping times from Japan to ensure that these were the first US models with the 'crocodile-eye' nose design that had reached other markets in the autumn of 2002.

The 2004 model WRX was introduced in May 2003, and the WRX STI made its North American debut a month or so later. STI's president revealed in an interview with *Road & Track* magazine that the WRX STI was specifically intended to counter US sales of the Mitsubishi Lancer Evo. For 2004 and later model-years, the WRX STI was based closely on the Japanese-market Spec C car, but of course with left-hand drive and the bigger 2.5-litre EJ257 engine. The 2004 cars also had a standard STI 15.2:1 steering rack instead of the Spec C car's 13:1 type.

Both WRX and WRX STI models had the inverted suspension struts and the same contoured seats. There was a new optional Premium Sedan Package, which incorporated an All Weather Package, a sunroof and rear spoiler. All WRX models now had the rev counter in the centre of the dash with the speedometer on the right.

2005 Models (Revision E)

The 2005 models went on sale through US dealers in May 2004, and there was a price increase from September. The new season's cars had no significant mechanical updates, but were distinguished by sill panels painted to match the body (instead of in black), black headlamp bezels with smoked-glass lenses, a single exhaust tailpipe and 16-inch alloy wheels with a grey finish that were borrowed from the US Legacy range. Less visibly, the rear suspension now had aluminium forward lateral links.

The WRX had an interior makeover, with a new centre console containing two cupholders (it was an industry joke at the time that cupholders sold cars to Americans). The armrests on the doors now contained controls for the electric mirrors, and there was a new automatic climate-control system with air filtration. The ICE system lost its cassette player and instead gained a six-CD changer and improved speakers. There was also a redesigned fob for the remote locking system.

WRX STI models shared these changes, and also gained an immobilizer. The wheels now had 8J rims and the rear wheel arches were slightly modified to give room for these. A new helical front differential replaced 2004's Suretrac type, and yaw sensors were added to feed information to the DCCD system.

June 2004 was also the time when the Impreza Sport Wagon first became available in the USA as a Saab 9-2X Aero, complete with WRX-style 227bhp 2-litre turbocharged engine and four-wheel drive. General Motors, Saab's US owners, needed a new model to fill a particular market niche, and reached agreement with Subaru that they could market a redesigned Sport Wagon with Saab badges. As a result, the car was given a redesigned nose and a number of other tweaks to make it fit the Swedish manufacturer's range more comfortably. Among those other tweaks were suspension refinements, which made the car less tiring to drive. They were so admired by the Subaru engineers that Saab's suspension chief stayed on in Japan after the 9-2X project was completed to help in further developments for the Impreza itself.

2006 Models (Revision F)

The 2006 US models arrived at the end of July 2005 and sported the new front-end design and the 230bhp 2.5-litre engine. This had the same Mitsubishi turbocharger as on the earlier 2.0-litre engines for the USA, but with the wastegate modified to open when boost pressure reached 1.0 bar. The cars were 50mm (2in) longer than before, up to 4447.75mm (175.8in) from 4397mm (173.8in).

There were now four turbocharged models. The three WRX types were the WRX TR (the TR stood for Tuner Ready), WRX, and WRX Limited (which replaced the earlier Premium saloon and could be had as a Sports Wagon as well). Only the Limited models could be had with automatic transmission. The fourth model was the WRX STI. (It was at this point that US publicity began to use a capital 'I' in the STI designation, having previously used a lower-case one.)

The 2006 WRX models also had new silver seven-spoke wheels with a 7Jx17 size, and fatter, 215/45ZR17 tyres. The front brakes now had larger 292mm ventilated discs with four-piston calipers, and the solid rear discs had a 262mm diameter and twin-piston calipers. All calipers were painted red with the Subaru name picked out in white. Saloons had aluminium lower A-arms on the front suspension, and the steering rack ratio was changed (to 15:1) to improve feel. Dual-ring synchromesh on first gear was introduced to reduce the notchy feel of the gearbox and improve downshifts from second to first gear.

Interior revisions included two-stage front airbags, side airbags, an outside temperature gauge and nets on the front seat backs. The WRX Limited came with leather upholstery, an electric sunroof, and the All Weather Package as standard.

The WRX STI models now had a black-finish aluminium rear roof spoiler, a lower-profile bonnet scoop, day-time running lights and a steering-wheel sensor, which had been added to improve the DCCD's response in cornering.

2007 Models (Revision G)
The 2007-model Imprezas reached US showrooms in August 2006, and among the changes were some new paint colours. The range consisted of WRX, WRX Limited, WRX STI, and WRX STI Limited models; the STI Limited was listed at the same price as the STI. The engine now had a completely new ECU, which had been re-mapped to meet US LEV2 emissions requirements (and went on to cause some timing and throttle problems). Cast-steel suspension arms replaced the aluminium-alloy components of earlier cars, apparently as a way of reducing costs on these final GD-series cars.

The base WRX model now had a new steering wheel and gear knob. The WRX STI gained a torsen limited-slip differential at the rear and a new lip spoiler for the boot lid, but lost the roof spoiler. It also had gold BBS-forged ten-spoke alloy wheels with gold brake calipers.

All models had some interior upgrades, with a leather-rimmed steering wheel, a 120-watt ICE with CD changer and auxiliary input port next to the cigarette lighter. They were also pre-wired for the Sirius satellite radio system available in the USA.

The 2007 STI Limited was a limited production run of 800 cars, all individually numbered and carrying a plaque on the dashboard. There were 400 in Satin White and 400 in Urban Grey, and they had painted silver 17-inch ten-spoke

alloy wheels made by Enkei, with black-painted brake calipers lettered in white with the Subaru name. An electrically operated glass sunroof and fog lights were standard; there was a deeper front lip spoiler and a small lip spoiler on the boot lid. The cabin featured leather upholstery with heated front seats and improved carpeting, plus darker metallic trim and an auto-dimming rear-view mirror that incorporated a digital compass readout. There was a new centre rear armrest and a hatch in the rear seat allowed long loads to be fed through from the boot.

The Oceania-Specification Imprezas

There are various conflicting definitions of the term 'Oceania', but for Japanese car manufacturers it generally means the Pacific Islands and Australasia. For Subaru, these constituted a self-contained sales area, although it embraced cars with both right-hand and left-hand drive. The notes below focus on the specification changes for the Australian cars.

Both saloons and Sports Wagons were sold in Australia, which was one of the few territories to take automatic-transmission derivatives of the WRX. These cost extra, and were not available for the 2001 season, when Australia received GD-series Revision A types. These had 215bhp (218PS) versions of the EJ205 2.0-litre engine, with 7Jx17 wheels, ventilated brake discs all round, four-piston front calipers and two-piston rears.

Automatic models became available on the Revision B models for 2002, which also gained a Suretrac limited-slip differential at the rear. To improve acceleration, the gear ratios were changed to those used on the Japanese-market WRX. The WRX STI also became available from December 2001, with 265bhp at 6000rpm and 253lb ft at 4000rpm. The 2003 model-year cars were Revision C types, and this year was a record for Subaru sales in Australia. As in North America, the Revision D facelift cars were introduced for the 2004 model-year, in effect a year behind Europe and Japan. Revision E (2005 model-year), Revision F (2006) and Revision G (2007) models followed, and broadly followed the pattern of their equivalents in other export markets.

Australia also had a series of limited-edition models, of which there are more details in Chapter 8. The most interesting of these were perhaps the Club Spec models, of which there was a new edition every year.

CHAPTER 7

THE RALLYING STORY, 2001–2007

The second-generation Imprezas ran in the Subaru World Rally Team throughout their production life, from 2001 to 2007. The competition in the WRC was even hotter than during the 1990s, and Subaru as a team did not do as well. Yet, although they never managed to win the WRC Manufacturers' Championship, their drivers shone in the rankings for the individual title. Subaru team drivers won the Drivers' Championship in both 2001 and 2003.

Once again, the cars were prepared by Prodrive, and that at least kept British WRC enthusiasts interested in the Subaru results. But after Richard Burns had left the team at the end of the 2001 season, there was no longer a world-class British driver in the SWRT, and interest dwindled somewhat as a result. It was very noticeable that, when Petter Solberg claimed the Drivers' Championship in 2003 and Subaru issued a special-edition car in his honour (see Chapter 8), the UK-market derivative did not carry the Solberg name.

During this period, many privateers also drove privately prepared WRX STI models in rallies, both those designated for the World series and others.

2001 SEASON

Events
Monte Carlo, 19–21 January
Sweden, 9–11 February
Portugal, 8–11 March
Spain, 23–25 March
Argentina, 3–6 May
Cyprus, 1–3 June
Acropolis (Greece), 15–17 June

Safari (Kenya), 20–22 July
1000 Lakes (Finland), 24–26 August
New Zealand, 21–23 September
San Remo, 4–7 October
Tour de Corse (Corsica), 19–21 October
Australia, 1–4 November
RAC (Wales Rally GB), 23–25 November

Drivers
Richard Burns/Robert Reid
Petter Solberg/Phil Mills
Markko Märtin/Michael Park
Toshihiro Arai/Glenn McNeall (Tony Sircombe co-drove on RAC Rally)

Cars

X1 SRT	X10 SRT
X2 SRT	X11 SRT
X3 SRT	X12 SRT
X4 SRT	X15 SRT
X5 SRT	X16 SRT
X6 SRT	X17 SRT
X7 SRT	X20 SRT
X8 SRT	X21 SRT
X9 SRT	X30 SRT

Podium Finishes
Argentina: Burns 2nd
Cyprus: Burns 2nd
Acropolis: Solberg 2nd
1000 Lakes: Burns 2nd
New Zealand: Burns 1st
Australia: Burns 2nd
RAC: Burns 3rd

2001 was the year when Richard Burns finally won the Drivers' Championship. Here he is on his way to second place in Australia.

Petter Solberg was pictured here on the 2001 Safari Rally. Like his two fellow drivers on that event, he was put out of action by suspension failure.

Overall Results
Subaru 4th in WRC Manufacturers' Championship.
Burns 1st in WRC Drivers' Championship.

Prodrive built at least 18 of the new GD-based cars for 2001, and these completely replaced the old GC-based models from the start of the rally season; it would never have done to rely on the old cars once the new model was firmly in the showrooms. They were of course based on the four-door body shell because there were no two-door Imprezas within the latest range, but a great deal of their construction and their main mechanical features were carried over from the WRC2000 cars.

The weight was all kept as low down as possible, and of course the cars retained the familiar Subaru rally colours of dark metallic blue with contrasting yellow decals on their flanks. Aerodynamics were said to have been improved, as was weight distribution, and the centre of gravity was now lower than ever. The cars had lost weight, too, and had to carry ballast to get them up to the minimum 1230kg (2706lb) demanded by the FIA regulations. Richard Burns automatically now became lead driver, and Petter Solberg became Subaru's number two. Subaru fielded at least three cars in every one of the season's 14 rounds, adding a fourth car for Portugal, Greece, San Remo, Corsica and the RAC Rally. This year's guest drivers were Markko Märtin (with co-driver Michael Park) and Toshihiro Arai (with Glenn MacNeall as co-driver in every event except the RAC, when Tony Sircombe did the honours).

Despite continual improvement to the cars during the season, it proved an enormously frustrating one. Burns lived up to his billing as the team's star driver with six podium finishes but achieved only a single first place, which was in New Zealand. Solberg had to be content with much poorer results, achieving only one podium finish. There were too many retirements all round: none of the three cars completed the Monte or the Safari; three of the four cars failed to finish in Portugal, Greece, and at San Remo; two of the three failed to finish in Catalunya; Solberg was out in Cyprus and Arai out in Corsica and Australia; and there were two retirements from the four cars entered in the RAC Rally.

Despite the ups and downs, Richard Burns' results were consistent enough to win him the Drivers' Championship. In the Manufacturers' Championship, however, Subaru dropped to fourth place. Sadly, Burns decided he needed

a change of scenery, and for 2002 he would be with the Peugeot team.

2002 SEASON

Events
Monte Carlo, 17–20 January
Sweden, 1–3 February
Tour de Corse (Corsica), 8–10 March
Spain, 21–24 March
Cyprus, 19–21 April
Argentina, 16–19 May
Acropolis (Greece), 13–16 June
Safari (Kenya), 12–14 July
1000 Lakes (Finland), 8–11 August
Rallye Deutschland (Germany), 22–25 August
San Remo, 19–22 September
New Zealand, 3–6 October
Australia, 31 October– 3 November
RAC (Wales Rally GB), 14–17 November

Drivers
Petter Solberg/Phil Mills
Toshihiro Arai/Tony Sircombe
Tommi Makinen/Kaj Lindstrom
Achim Mörtl/Klaus Wicha

Cars

X2 SRT	X28 SRT
X9 SRT	PR02 SRT
X12 SRT	PS02 SRT
X21 SRT	PS02 SSS
X23 SRT	PT02 SRT
X24 SRT	TM02 SRT
X26 SRT	TM02 SSS
X27 SRT	

Podium Finishes
Monte Carlo: Makinen 1st
Cyprus: Makinen 3rd
Argentina: Solberg 2nd
1000 Lakes: Solberg 3rd
San Remo: Solberg 3rd
New Zealand: Makinen 3rd
Australia: Solberg 3rd
RAC: Solberg 1st

Preparing the Cars

Rally cars take a huge amount of punishment, and the body shell of every Impreza run by the SWRT was completely rebuilt before an event. Those rebuilds became progressively more and more demanding. Subaru have revealed that a body-shell rebuild took 650 man-hours in 2003, but that by 2006 no fewer than 780 man-hours went into each rebuild. That was one reason why the number of cars prepared for the SWRT increased over the years: with events following one another thick and fast, there was often not enough time to rebuild cars between one WRC round and the next.

On an event, major damage has to be repaired quickly. By the time of the WRC2007 cars, transmission and differential cases were made of magnesium alloy in order to save weight. Engines, transmissions and differentials were all built up as oil-sealed units, so that they could be swapped very quickly at a service stop: Subaru quoted a typical time of 10–12 minutes for a major component change in 2007.

Costs were of course far beyond those associated with the road cars. Of the WRC2007 cars, Subaru claimed that it took 85 hours to build each transmission, at a cost of more than £75,000. The unique centre differential and modifications to the front and rear differentials demanded 16 hours of build time and the total cost for that was around £20,000.

The WRC cars also had a semi-automatic gearshift with electronic control and hydraulic actuation. The hydraulic system operated at 2500psi, and was capable of effecting a gear change in 0.1 seconds. This was vital on a rally, when a missed gear change could see engine revs rise to catastrophic levels and put a car out of action.

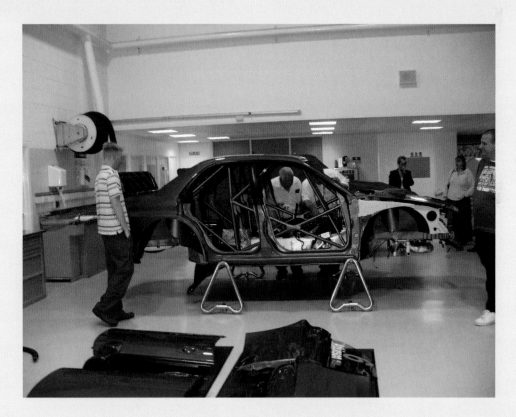

Chris Atkinson's car being prepared by Prodrive in 2006. (Wikimedia Commons)

Makinen drove hard in the 2002 Australian event, but was disqualified for driving without a spare wheel.

Petter Solberg on the Spanish event – the 555 sponsorship decals returned to the cars for 2002.

Overall Results
Subaru 3rd in WRC Manufacturers' Championship
Solberg 2nd in WRC Drivers' Championship
Makinen 8th in WRC Drivers' Championship

Subaru started the 2002 season using the WRC2001 cars, introducing the new WRC2002 models for the Tour de Corse in March. They looked much like the 2001 cars, but British American Tobacco had once again agreed to sponsor the team, and the cars now carried '555' decals on their flanks, as they had in the past. There would be continual development throughout the season. The turbocharger, driveshafts, transmission housing and steering column would all be modified, and the exhaust manifold would also change from a four-into-two-into-one type to a simpler four-into-one configuration. No less than 33lb was shaved off the weight by modifying brackets, wiring and glass.

To replace Richard Burns, Subaru managed to secure the services of Tommi Makinen, a four-times winner of the Drivers' Championship. With Petter Solberg remaining faithful to the Impreza, it looked like being a good year. Guest drivers were Toshihiro Arai (with co-driver Tony Sircombe) on the Acropolis and Rallye Deutschland, and Achim Mörtl (with Klaus Wicha) in Germany and San Remo.

Makinen got off to a good start with victory in the Monte, but after that his best results were third places in Cyprus and New Zealand, fourth on the RAC Rally, and sixth in Finland and Germany. He managed to write off two cars, one in Corsica and the other in Argentina, was obliged to retire with damaged cars in Sweden, Spain, Greece, Kenya and San Remo, and was disqualified in Australia for driving an under-weight car after abandoning his spare wheel.

Solberg was much more consistent, finishing in nine of the 14 events. He achieved five podium places, closing the season with a win in the RAC Rally. His other results were a second in Argentina, third places in Finland, San Remo and Australia, a heroic fifth in Cyprus after early throttle failure, and sixth on the Monte. In Sweden, Corsica, Greece, Kenya and New Zealand he was unable to finish.

Solberg finished the season second in the Drivers' Championship, but a long way behind winner Marcus Grönholm of the Peugeot team. Subaru was stuck at fourth in the Manufacturers' Championship once again.

2003 SEASON

Events
Monte Carlo, 24–26 January
Sweden, 7–9 February
Turkey, 27 February–3 March
New Zealand, 10–12 April
Argentina, 8–11 May
Acropolis (Greece), 6–8 June
Cyprus, 19–21 June
Rallye Deutschland (Germany), 25–27 July
1000 Lakes (Finland), 7–10 August
Australia, 4–7 September
San Remo, 3–5 October
Tour de Corse (Corsica), 17–19 October
Catalunya (Spain), 24–26 October
RAC (Wales Rally GB), 6–9 November

Drivers
Petter Solberg/Phil Mills
Tommi Makinen/Kaj Lindstrom

Cars

S30 WRT	S100 WRT
S40 WRT	S200 WRT
S50 WRT	S300 WRT
S60 WRT	S400 WRT
S70 WRT	S500 WRT
S80 WRT	S600 WRT
S90 WRT	S700 WRT

Podium Finishes
Sweden: Makinen 2nd
New Zealand: Solberg 3rd
Acropolis (Greece): Solberg 3rd
Cyprus: Solberg 1st
1000 Lakes (Finland): Solberg 2nd
Australia: Solberg 1st
Tour de Corse (Corsica): Solberg 1st
RAC: Solberg 1st

Overall Results
Subaru 3rd in WRC Manufacturers' Championship
Solberg 1st in WRC Drivers' Championship
Makinen 8th in WRC Drivers' Championship

For 2003 there was another all-new set of team cars, now

Subaru UK released a press picture in 2003 to suggest how closely the WRX STI and WRC cars were related. In practice, there were very many differences under the skin.

Petter Solberg came a disappointing fifth in Argentina in 2003.

Solberg's drive in Greece was much more successful, and was rewarded with a third place.

featuring the facelifted nose that had been designed in double-quick time by Peter Stevens. Strangely, though, there were no 555 logos on them this year, even though BAT's sponsorship was in place again. The body shells were even lighter and stiffer than before, and torque at lower engine speeds had been boosted by changes to the turbocharger and elsewhere. Throughout the year, changes were being made to the suspension of the cars, but overall it was more reliable than it had been.

Subaru retained both Petter Solberg (in car number 7) and Tommi Makinen (in car number 8) as their drivers, which made for welcome continuity. But the two could not have had more different seasons. Solberg failed to finish three times, running out of fuel in San Remo, going off in the Monte and breaking a steering arm in Turkey. He was eighth in Germany, sixth in Sweden, and fifth in Argentina and Spain, but seven strong podium places ensured 2003 would be a good season for him. He was third in New Zealand and Greece, second in Finland, and placed first in Cyprus, Australia, Corsica and the RAC Rally. The points stacked up and he finished the season with the World Drivers' Championship title, just one point ahead of Citroën driver Sebastien Loeb.

Makinen's year was more disappointing. He failed to finish in four events and finished too far down in too many others for his own comfort. He was tenth in San Remo, eighth in Spain and Turkey, seventh in New Zealand and Corsica, sixth in Finland and Australia, and fifth on the Acropolis. Only on the RAC Rally and in Sweden did he show his old form, finishing third and second respectively in these events. His points left him eighth in the Drivers' Championship ranking, and it was an unhappy Makinen who decided to retire from WRC competition completely at the end of the season.

Subaru, meanwhile, moved up one position in the Constructors' Championship, to third.

2004 SEASON

Events
Monte Carlo, 23–25 January
Sweden, 6–8 February
Mexico, 12–14 March
New Zealand, 16–18 April
Cyprus, 14–16 May
Acropolis (Greece), 14–16 June

Turkey, 25–27 June
Argentina, 16–18 July
1000 Lakes (Finland), 6–8 August
Rallye Deutschland (Germany), 20–22 August
Japan, 3–5 September
RAC (Wales Rally GB), 17–19 September
Italy, 1–3 October
Tour de Corse (Corsica), 15–17 October
Catalunya (Spain), 29–31 October
Australia, 12–14 November

Drivers
Petter Solberg/Phil Mills
Mikko Hirvonen/Jarno Lehtinen
Stéphane Sarrazin/Patrick Pivato

Cars
555 WRC	JT53 SRT
S30 WRT	LT53 SRT
S90 WRT	MT53 SRT
S400 WRT	NT53 SRT
S800 WRT	OT53 SRT
S900 WRT	RT53 SRT
AT53 SRT	ST53 SRT
CT53 SRT	YT53 SRT

Podium Finishes
Sweden: Solberg 3rd
New Zealand: Solberg 1st
Acropolis: Solberg 1st
Turkey: Solberg 3rd

The 2004 WRC Imprezas looked much like those used in 2003, but inevitably there were many invisible changes.

New Zealand in 2004 saw Petter Solberg win one of the titles that contributed to his second place in the Drivers' Championship.

Solberg did not finish the Australian event in 2004, although clearly not for want of trying!

Japan: Solberg 1st
RAC: Solberg 1st
Italy: Solberg 1st

Overall Results
Subaru 3rd in WRC Manufacturers' Championship
Solberg 2nd in WRC Drivers' Championship

Subaru started the 2004 rally season with the 2003 season's cars, introducing the WRC2004 cars in mid-March on the third round in Mexico. The new cars had few cosmetic changes, but new project manager Ed Wood had made use of lightweight materials permitted by a new FIA rule change. Body panels, aerodynamics, electronic control systems, suspension and engine had all come in for attention, and half-way through the season there was a revised gearbox as well.

Number-one driver was Petter Solberg, and the new man on the team was Mikko Hirvonen, fresh from the Ford team and partnered by co-driver Jarno Lehtinen. Guest crew Stéphane Sarrazin and Patrick Pivato drove with sponsorship from Subaru France on three events, in Germany, Corsica and Spain, where they finished ninth, sixth and fourth respectively.

Hirvonen's season was not very successful. He failed to finish in four events (the Monte, the Acropolis, Finland and Italy) and did not achieve a single podium place. There was a tenth in Corsica, a ninth in Sweden, eighth places in Germany and Spain, seventh places in New Zealand, Japan, and on the RAC, a sixth in Turkey, fifth places in Mexico and Cyprus, and his best placings were fourth in Argentina and Australia. Hirvonen was not asked to drive for Subaru again in 2005.

World champion Petter Solberg should have had a better season, but the Ford and Peugeot teams were just too strong, and kept the Subarus at arm's length. Solberg was unlucky in Mexico, which he might have won but for a controversial penalty meted out when spectators helped push his car to a service point. He was also unlucky in Germany, where he hit a bridge in spectacular fashion and was lucky to escape with relatively minor injuries. He did not finish in Argentina, Finland or Australia, either. The Monte saw him in seventh place, there were fifth places in Corsica and Spain, and the Solberg car came fourth in Mexico and Cyprus. But seven podium finishes kept Solberg well up in the points championship, and he finished the season in second place, albeit with a large gap of 32 points between

him and winner Sébastien Loeb from the Citroën team. Solberg finished third in Sweden and Turkey, but racked up no fewer than five victories, in New Zealand, Greece, Japan, on the Rally GB, and in Italy.

2005 SEASON

Events
Monte Carlo, 21–23 January
Sweden, 11–13 February
Mexico, 11–13 March
New Zealand, 8–10 April
Italy, 29 April–1 May
Cyprus, 13–15 May
Turkey, 3–5 June
Acropolis (Greece), 24–26 June
Argentina, 15–17 July
1000 Lakes (Finland), 5–7 August
Rallye Deutschland (Germany), 26–28 August
RAC (Wales Rally GB), 16–18 September

Mexico, March 2005: Solberg on his way to a win.

The 2005 Monte was less successful for Solberg – he did not finish.

Japan, 30 September–2 October
Tour de Corse (Corsica), 21–23 October
Catalunya (Spain), 28–30 October
Australia, 11–13 November

Drivers
Petter Solberg/Phil Mills
Stéphane Sarrazin/Denis Giraudet
Chris Atkinson/Glenn McNeall

Cars

RT53 SRT	GC54 WRC
ST53 SRT	HC54 WRC
WT53 SRT	JC54 WRC
AC54 WRC	LC54 WRC
BC54 WRC	MC54 WRC
CC54 WRC	NC54 WRC
EC54 WRC	OU04 XNZ

Podium Finishes
Sweden: Solberg 1st

Mexico: Solberg 1st
New Zealand: Solberg 3rd
Italy: Solberg 2nd
Turkey: Solberg 2nd
Argentina: Solberg 3rd
RAC: Solberg 1st
Japan: Atkinson 3rd
Tour de Corse: Solberg 3rd

Overall Results
Subaru 4th in WRC Manufacturers' Championship
Solberg 2nd in WRC Drivers' Championship

Subaru used 2004 cars for the first two rounds of the 2005 season, and introduced the WRC2005 for the Mexico Rally in March. The new cars had stiffer body shells that were 30mm (1.2in) wider to cover widened tracks. They also had a larger number of composite body panels, including the front and rear wings and bumpers, to save weight. There had been suspension and aerodynamic tweaks, too, and the engines had lightened flywheels, a revised IHI turbocharger, and modified water-injection and fuel-injection systems. While peak power remained 300bhp at 5000rpm, maximum torque was now 435lb ft, generated at 4000rpm.

Solberg remained faithful to Subaru, and was naturally the team's lead driver in car number 5. The number-two driver for this year was Stéphane Sarrazin, the French driver who had enjoyed a few outings for Subaru in 2004 and was now teamed with Denis Giraudet, who had formerly been Didier Auriol's co-driver. There was a third driver, too, and Australian Chris Atkinson competed in a number of rounds with Glenn McNeall as co-driver.

Solberg put in another strong showing, which netted him joint second place in the drivers' rankings, although yet again a long way behind leader Loeb. Although he did not finish in the Monte, Cyprus, Japan or Australia, and came a disappointing 13th in Catalunya, ninth on the Acropolis, and seventh in Germany, his other results were very respectable indeed. There was a fourth in Finland, third places in New Zealand, Argentina and Corsica, second places in Italy and Turkey, and wins in Sweden and Mexico.

Sarrazin's season was altogether more disappointing. He failed to finish on the RAC Rally or in Spain, and was ranked 14th on the Monte, 13th in Sweden and on the Acropolis, 12th in Italy, and 8th in Germany. His best result was a fourth place in Corsica.

Chris Atkinson's results were also erratic. He did not finish in Mexico, Corsica, Finland or on the Acropolis. The RAC Rally saw him come a miserable 38th; he was 24th in Turkey, 19th in Sweden and 18th in Italy. In Germany he was 11th, in Cyprus tenth, in Spain and Argentine ninth, in New Zealand seventh, and in Australia fourth. His sole podium finish was in Japan, where he came third.

Despite Solberg's efforts, it proved another frustrating year for Subaru. They dropped one place down the manufacturers' rankings again, to fourth.

2006 SEASON

Events
Monte Carlo, 19–22 January
Sweden, 3–5 February
Mexico, 3–5 March
Catalunya (Spain), 24–26 March
Tour de Corse (Corsica), 7–9 April

Chris Atkinson was the number two Subaru driver for 2006, and finished ninth in Australia.

Petter Solberg achieved Subaru's only podium placings in 2006, although he did not finish in the Finnish event. The cars were new for the season, with the latest three-element grille design.

Argentina, 28–30 April
Sardinia, 19–21 May
Acropolis (Greece), 2–4 June
Rallye Deutschland (Germany), 11–13 August
Finland, 17–20 August
Japan, 1–3 September
Cyprus, 22–24 September
Turkey, 13–15 October
Australia, 26–29 October
New Zealand, 17–19 November
RAC (Wales Rally GB), 1–3 December

Drivers
Petter Solberg/Phil Mills
Stéphane Sarrazin/Jacques Renucci
Chris Atkinson/Glenn McNeall
Toshihiro Arai/Tony Sircombe

Cars
FT55 SRT   CT06 SRT
BT06 SRT   and others

Podium Finishes
Mexico: Solberg 2nd
Argentina: Solberg 2nd

Australia: Solberg 2nd
Wales Rally GB: Solberg 3rd

Overall Results
Subaru 3rd in WRC Manufacturers' Championship
Solberg 6th in WRC Drivers' Championship

The FIA rule changes introduced for the 2006 WRC season were the most-far-reaching since the introduction of the WRC formula in 1997. Active differentials and water injection were now banned, and teams were obliged to re-use cars and engines on selected pairs of events. As a result, Subaru, like every other competing team, had to run its WRC2006 cars from the opening event in Monte Carlo.

Petter Solberg was again the team's lead driver, supported by Chris Atkinson in the second car except on tarmac events, when Stéphane Sarrazin stepped in. But a failure to score in the first two rounds led to a shake-up at Prodrive. Team boss David Lapworth, who had run the SWRT for ten years, stepped down and Paul Howarth took over. The whole season proved disappointing for Subaru, with the team failing to achieve a single win and ending up on the podium only four times. The Citroën and Ford teams remained unassailable leaders of the pack, and it was beginning to look as if the Impreza's star was on the wane even though Subaru did creep up the manufacturers' ranking by one place to finish third. The failure was felt keenly in the Subaru camp. In a TV documentary about the team's WRC campaign that year, called Engineering the World Rally, 2006 was remembered as 'the season from Hell'.

It was Petter Solberg who achieved every one of those few podium placings, with a third at the Wales Rally GB and seconds in Mexico, Argentina and Australia. He did not finish on the Monte, or in Sweden, Germany or Finland. Turkey brought him a 13th place, Corsica an 11th, and Italy a ninth. In Cyprus he came eighth, he was seventh in Spain, Greece and Japan, and New Zealand saw him finish in sixth place. Although the points added up to give him sixth place in the Drivers' Championship, it was a disappointing result for a man who had been World Champion only three years earlier.

Chris Atkinson posted two 13th places, in Corsica and Finland, three eleventh placings, in Sweden, Spain and Greece, a tenth in Italy, ninth in Cyprus and Australia, eighth in Germany, seventh in Mexico and sixth places in Turkey, Argentina, on the Monte and in the Rally GB. He did not finish in New Zealand, and his best result was fourth in Japan.

Sarrazin did not finish in Germany, posted eighth places in Catalunya and Corsica, and was fifth on the Monte.

2007 SEASON

Events
Monte Carlo, 19–21 January
Sweden, 9–11 February
Norway, 16–18 February
Mexico, 9–11 March
Portugal, 30 March–1 April
Argentina, 4–6 May
Sardinia, 18–20 May
Acropolis (Greece), 1–3 June
Finland, 3–5 August
Rallye Deutschland (Germany), 17–19 August
New Zealand, 31 August–2 September
Catalunya (Spain), 5–7 October
Tour de Corse (Corsica), 12–14 October
Japan, 26–28 October
Ireland, 16–18 November
RAC (Wales Rally GB), 30 November–2 December

Drivers
Petter Solberg/Phil Mills
Chris Atkinson/Glenn McNeall (first five rallies) and Stéphane Prévot (remainder)
Xavier Pons/Xavier Amigo

Cars

FT56 SRT	JY07 SRT
JT56 SRT	and others

Podium Finishes
Portugal: Solberg 2nd
Acropolis: Solberg 3rd

Overall Results
Subaru 3rd in WRC Manufacturers' Championship
Solberg 5th in WRC Drivers' Championship
Atkinson 7th in WRC Drivers' Championship

The 2007 WRC Imprezas looked very similar to the previous year's cars, and were revealed to the media on 2 March, just a week before the Rally of Mexico was due to start. Engine work had been focused on reducing weight,

What Were They Called?

Subaru identified its second-generation Impreza WRC cars by names that incorporated digits identifying the rally season for which they were built. The list is as follows:

2001 season	WRC2001
2002 season	WRC2002
2003 season	WRC2003
2004 season	WRC2004
2005 season	WRC2005
2006 season	WRC2006
2007 season	WRC2007

Prodrive used different names for these cars, as follows:

2001 season	S7
2002 season	S8
2003 season	S9
2004 season	S10
2005 season	S11
2006 season	S12
2007 season	S12b

and there was now a new intercooler design with a turbo air inlet that passed through the bonnet scoop. Recent FIA rulings about aerodynamics had led to a number of apertures on the front and side of the body being partially blanked off, and airflow from under the bonnet now emerged through vents on the side rather than in the middle of the bonnet. The exhaust had also been moved, to emerge through the rear bumper.

The cars also had a new hydraulic control system for the centre differential, which was said to improve its effectiveness. A lot of work had also gone into balancing tyre wear more evenly, while weight distribution, dampers, suspension and differentials had all received attention.

Once again, Petter Solberg was the senior driver, with car number 7, and Chris Atkinson had the number-two position with car number 8. Xavier Pons joined the team in a third car, although this one was not nominated for

2007 was another frustrating year for Subaru. Xavier Pons finished sixth in Finland.

Petter Solberg's best result in 2007 was in Portugal, where he claimed second place.

Manufacturers' Championship points. His car carried number 25.

Yet again it was a disappointing season for Subaru; Solberg's co-driver Phil Mills called it 'the second season from Hell'. The team finished the season with no victories and only two podium finishes – both down to Solberg. Placings as far down as 42nd (Atkinson in Ireland, a new rally in the WRC) and 36th (Pons in Japan) were not what Subaru had come to expect. The only light on the horizon was that a brand-new rally car was just around the corner. The 2007 season would be the last one for the GD-series Imprezas.

The full list of results makes rather depressing reading. Even Petter Solberg had to be content with a rash of fourth, fifth and sixth placings, although his third in Greece and second in Portugal were highlights. Chris Atkinson's best results were fourth places on the Monte, in Finland and in New Zealand; his co-driver Glenn MacNeall left the team in mid-season, to be replaced by Stéphane Prévot, who had previously partnered Bruno Thiry in an Impreza. Pons, meanwhile, could do no better than a sixth place in Finland. Solberg posted five retirements in 15 events, Atkinson two, and Pons retired from one of the 12 events for which he was entered, failing to start in another.

Behind the Wheel: The Subaru WRC Drivers, 2001–2007

Toshihiro ARAI
'Toshi' Arai is a Japanese rally driver who made his debut in 1987. He drove Group N Imprezas for Subaru from 1997–2000 and 2002–2003, switching briefly to the Group A championship in 2000–2001. He subsequently founded his own team, called Subaru Team Arai, and in 2005 and 2007 drove WRX STI Imprezas to win the drivers' title in the Production Car World Rally Championship.

Chris ATKINSON
Australian Chris Atkinson drove for the Subaru team from 2005 to 2008. After making his name in Australia as a privateer, he secured a seat with the Suzuki team in the 2003 Asia-Pacific Rally Championship. He drove an Impreza WRX STI in the 2004 Rally New Zealand, and was signed to drive for the Subaru works team the following year. After Subaru pulled out of the WRC in 2008, Atkinson signed for the new Citroen Junior Team and has since driven for Proton and Skoda.

Richard BURNS
Richard Burns drove for Subaru in 2001, the year he won his World Championship title. For more details, see Chapter 4.

Mikko HIRVONEN
Finn Hirvonen first attracted attention when he won his class in the 2002 Finnish Rally Championship. Ford snapped him up for their 2003 WRC team, and just a year later he was driving for Subaru. After a disappointing season, Hirvonen became a privateer for 2005, and by 2006 was back with Ford. For 2012, he switched again, this time joining the Citroën team.

Tommi MÄKINEN
Tommi Mäkinen was a hugely respected rally driver before he came to Subaru in 2002. He started his career in his native Finland in 1988, and joined the Mitsubishi WRC team in 1995, remaining there until the end of the

2001 season. Between 1996 and 1999, he won the drivers' title every year. He stayed with Subaru for two years, but decided to retire from the sport at the end of 2003.

Markko MÄRTIN
Märtin joined Subaru in 2000 and remained in the WRC team for 2001. For further details, see Chapter 4.

Achim MÖRTL
Austrian driver Achim Mörtl began his career in 1993 with Toyota in the Austrian Rally Championship, and was Austrian Champion in 1996, 1999 and 2006. He drove for Subaru as a guest driver in two events during 2002. Mörtl retired from competitive motorsport in 2007 and has since worked as a rally coach.

Xavier PONS
Catalonian driver Xavier 'Xevi' Pons began his motorsport career on motorcycles and had become a world-class rider before switching to car rallying in 2002. By 2006 he was driving for Kronos Total Citroën, but was without a drive in 2007. He was planning to retire from the sport until Subaru offered him a drive in the third 2007 car. Although he was expected to remain in the team for 2008, in practice he focused on Spanish national rallies instead.

Stéphane SARRAZIN
French driver Sarrazin initially made his name with Peugeot and Minardi in Formula One, switching to rallying in 2004 when he signed with Subaru. He remained with the team in 2005, but then moved on to Peugeot in 2007 to drive in the Le Mans series, and has subsequently become a World Endurance Championship driver.

Petter SOLBERG
Petter Solberg was Subaru's longest-serving driver during the GD-series era, having joined in 2000 and remaining until Subaru withdrew from WRC events at the end of 2008. For more details, see Chapter 4.

CHAPTER 8

SPECIAL EDITIONS OF THE SECOND-GENERATION CARS, 2000–2007

UK SPECIAL EDITIONS

UK300 (2001)

300 Examples

This was the first UK special edition based on the second-generation Impreza, and the only one based on the 'bug-eye' variant. Performance was claimed to be 0–60mph in 5.9 seconds, with a maximum of 230km/h (143mph). It was announced on 23 May 2001 and cost £24,995.

Bodywork:
WR Blue Mica paint.
WRC-style headlights (gloss black shells with twin high-intensity Hella light units and indicators inset above).
Clear lenses for indicator repeaters and side markers.
Black front lip spoiler.
Special rear spoiler with Prodrive logo.
UK300 decal badges.

Interior:
Blue alcantara upholstery with matching door panels.
Floor mats with UK300 logo.
Numbered special edition plaque.

Engine:
1994cc engine with 215bhp at 5600rpm and 215lb ft at 3600rpm.
Optional Prodrive Performance Pack (£1600): remapped engine ECU, uprated intercooler piping and free-flow exhaust with different centre and rear sections including a big-bore tailpipe and giving 245bhp at 5600rpm and 261lb ft at 4000rpm.

Suspension:
Standard suspension.
18-inch x 7.5J ten-spoke Prodrive-OZ wheels with gold finish.
Pirelli Rosso P-Zero 225/40ZR18 tyres.

WR1 (2004)

500 examples

The WR1 was the UK derivative of a 1000-strong world-wide limited edition produced on the back of Petter Solberg's WRC win. All were based on the 2004-model Impreza WRX STI, but the UK cars were additionally modified by Prodrive. These cars had a 0–60mph time of 4.25 seconds and an electronically limited maximum speed of 250km/h (155mph). The WR1 limited edition was announced in January 2004 with a price of £29,995.

Bodywork:
Ice Blue metallic paint.
Special wing decal badges.
Mesh grille in stainless steel.

Interior:
Anthracite alcantara upholstery.
Special gear knob.
Special carpets.
DCCD control switch for front-to-rear torque split bias next to handbrake.

THIS PAGE AND OVERLEAF: *The 2001 UK300 limited edition was the only one based on the early second-generation 'bug-eye' models. Arguably, the black lamp bodies made a big improvement to the looks.*

Mechanical:
1994cc engine, with 315bhp at 5800rpm and 420Nm (309lb ft) at 4000rpm.
Prodrive Performance Pack (at this stage the PPP was not EU-homologated, and so was fitted after the car was registered).
DCCD (Driver Controlled Centre Differential).

Special exhaust system (not EU-homologated, and therefore fitted after the car was registered).

Suspension:
Prodrive WRX STi springs.
18-inch Prodrive PFF7 Pewter wheels.
Pirelli P-Zero 225/45ZR18 tyres.

THIS PAGE AND OVERLEAF: *Outside the UK, the 2004 special edition celebrating Petter Solberg's 2003 WRC win was named after the drive; in the UK, the cars were further modified by Prodrive and became the WR1 edition.*

WRX 300 (2005)

300 Examples
Introduced in late May 2005, this limited edition came with the Prodrive Performance Pack. Claimed performance figures were 0–60mph in 4.8 seconds and a maximum of more than 233km/h (145mph); some sources claim 243km/h (151mph). The original showroom price was £21,495.

Bodywork:
Blue Mica paint.
Fog-lamp covers with Subaru World Rally Team logos.
Optional special edition rear spoiler.

Interior:
Front bucket seats with Subaru World Rally Team logo.
Aluminium gear knob.
Carpet mats with WRX logo.
Anti-theft tracking device (RAC Trackstar; 12-month subscription included in price).

Engine:
1994cc engine with 265PS (261bhp) and 348Nm (257lb ft).
Prodrive Performance Package.

Running gear:
17-inch five-spoke gold alloy wheels with 215/45 tyres.
Optional sports suspension.
Optional Prodrive front brakes.
Optional 18-inch P-FF7 wheels.

Spec D (2006)

300 Examples
This was intended as a more discreet derivative of the STI for older customers. Performance was claimed to be 0–60mph in 5 seconds, with an electronically limited top speed of 250km/h (155mph). It was introduced in March 2006 and cost £28,495.

Bodywork:
Crystal Grey Metallic paint.
Projector-style fog lights.
Prodrive lower front grille.

The 2005 WRX300 limited edition returned to the familiar Blue Mica colour.

THIS PAGE AND OVERLEAF: *For would-be owners who thought the full-house WRX STI a little too garish, the 2006 Spec D limited edition offered the driving thrills with toned-down looks. A similar marketing tactic had been used in other countries.*

No roof spoiler.
Standard WRX boot spoiler (lower than STI type).

Interior:
Leather upholstery and door trims in black.
Automatic climate control.
Extra sound insulation.
SmartNav satnav system with touch-screen operation.
Pioneer DEH-P70BT 200-watt ICE head unit with iPod adapter and Bluetooth phone connection.
Anti-theft tracking device (RAC Trackstar; 12-month subscription included in price).

Engine:
1994cc engine, with 276 bhp.

Running gear:
Standard suspension.
Silver-finish 10-spoke wheels.

RB320 (2007)

320 Examples
The RB320 was released in November 2006, a year after the death of former Subaru WRC driver Richard Burns, whose initials were represented in the name of the car. The 320 stood for the power output (in PS) and also for the number of examples produced. The car was based on an Impreza WRX STI and had the Prodrive Performance Package. Claimed performance figures were 0–60mph in 4.8 seconds, 1–100mph in 12.2 seconds, and the estimated maximum was 250km/h 155mph.

Early customers were invited to a special launch event in March 2007 at the Prodrive test track in Warwickshire. They could take delivery of their cars at the circuit, drive demonstration STIs around the track, and meet rally celebrities. It was possible to register online as a buyer and to reserve the limited-edition number of choice through a special sub-section of the Subaru website. Subaru (UK) Ltd also donated a car to be raffled through Autosport magazine; the proceeds of the raffle went to the Richard Burns Foundation to support those suffering from serious injury or illness.

Bodywork:
Obsidian Black paint.
Chrome mesh grille.
Front lip spoiler.
Special RB320 badges.

The RB320 was the second UK limited edition named after Richard Burns, who had died of cancer in 2006. The all-black paint was appropriate.

Interior:
Quickshift gear change.
Side sill plates.
RB320 logo on gear knob.
RB320 logo on carpet mats.
Individually numbered tax disc holder in black alloy.
Optional black leather and alcantara upholstery with stitched RB320 logo on the seats, and a special gear knob.

Mechanical:
2457cc engine, with 320PS (316bhp) at 6000rpm and 450Nm (332lb ft) at 3700rpm.
Prodrive Performance Pack.

Suspension:
Prodrive suspension with Eibach springs and rear anti-roll bar, and Bilstein damper struts.
Ride height lowered by 30mm (1.2in) at the front and 10mm (0.4in) at the rear.
18-inch alloy wheels with Anthracite finish.

GB270 (2007)

300 Saloons, 100 Sports Wagons
The 400-strong GB270 special edition was based on the WRX and named after its 270PS engine, the GB standing for Great Britain. Claimed performance was 0–60mph in 4.9 seconds with a 235km/h (146mph) maximum; the top speed was lower than that of other models because the car had the Prodrive five-speed gearbox with Quickshift instead of the six-speed that was then standard. The cars cost £22,995 each and were released in August 2007.

Bodywork:
World Rally Blue Mica (four-door saloon) or Urban Grey Metallic (five-door Sports Wagon).
Prodrive polished stainless-steel mesh front grille (saloon) or black grilles (Sports Wagon).

Interior:
Special floor mats
Special badges.

ABOVE AND BELOW: *The GB270 was the last limited edition based on the second-generation turbocharged Impreza, and could be had as a saloon or as a five-door estate.*

'Unofficial' UK Limited Editions

Two 'unofficial' limited editions were created by Litchfield Imports, a Gloucestershire company that still specializes in importing Subaru models that are not otherwise available in the UK.

Litchfield Type 25 (2004)

Litchfield created this car when Subaru modified the specification of the Japanese Spec C models they had been importing by deleting such items as electric windows and air conditioning. As a replacement, Litchfield created their own specification by fitting modified US-specification EJ257 2.5-litre engines into Japanese-specification STi cars.

The cylinder heads were modified to deliver 350bhp. Suspension was modified with rebound adjustable AST Sportline I struts, Whiteline anti-roll bars and an anti-lift kit.

Litchfield Type 25 (2007)

The second Litchfield Type 25 was based on a 2007-specification Japanese Spec C car. Like the earlier Type 25, it had a modified EJ257 cylinder block, this time modified with the aid of the US arm of Cosworth.

A modified STI crankshaft and STI engine casing were used in tandem with balanced Cosworth forged pistons and rods. The heads used larger valves and special camshafts developed by Cosworth. The results were power of 415bhp and torque of 569Nm (420lb ft).

Momo gear knob.
Optional leather or alcantara-and-leather upholstery, in each case with GB270 logos (£1400 extra on saloon or £1600 extra on Sports Wagon).
Optional ICE Pack (£1750) of Clarion satellite navigation system, iPod adapter and Bluetooth phone kit.

Engine:
2457cc engine, with 270PS (266bhp) and 420Nm (310lb ft).

Prodrive Performance Pack.

Running gear:
Five-speed gearbox with Quickshift.
Suspension lowered by 30mm (1.2in) in front and by 10mm (0.4in) at rear.
Prodrive anti-roll bar.
18-inch Prodrive alloy wheels, silver on four-door or black on five-door.

JAPANESE SPECIAL EDITIONS

S202 (2002)

400 Examples
The S202 was announced in May 2002 for a June start to sales, and was another rapid success for Subaru, with all 400 examples selling within two weeks. The car was based on the WRX STI Type RA Spec C.

Bodywork:
Astral Yellow, Midnight Black Mica, Pure White, or WR Blue Mica.
Projector headlights.
Carbon-fibre rear wing.
Fog-lamp covers (but no lights).
S202 logos front and rear.

Interior:
Blue dial faces.
Aluminium pedals.
Black upholstery with STI logo.
Special finish for centre console and door trims.
Numbered special-edition plaque.

Engine:
2457cc engine, with 320bhp at 6400rpm and 283lb ft at 4400rpm.
8.0:1 compression ratio.
Modified ECU.
Silicone inlet ducting.
Lightweight air conditioning compressor.
Exhaust system with titanium elements to save approx 5kg (11lb).
Aluminium oil cooler behind front number-plate.

Running gear:
'Pillow-ball' joints in rear suspension links.
Lightweight grooved brake discs.
Stainless braided brake hoses.
Gold 10-spoke RAYS 17-inch alloy wheels with STI logos.
Pirelli P-Zero Rosso tyres.

S203 (2005)

555 Examples
This special-edition Impreza was announced in December 2004. It was based on the WRX STI and incorporated a large number of items from the STI catalogue. Production ran from January to March 2005, and the base price was 4,609,500 yen, including sales tax.

Bodywork:
Crystal Grey Metallic, Pure White, Solid Red or WR Blue Mica paint.
Tinted windows.
HID low-beam headlights.
Fog-lamp covers with STI decals.
Carbon-fibre front lip spoiler.
Rubber extension to front lip spoiler.
Silver mesh grille.
S203 grille and tail badges.
Two-way adjustable rear wing spoiler.

Interior:
Recaro carbon-fibre reclining front bucket seats.
Grey alcantara upholstery and door panels.
Black floor mats.
Black soft-feel coating on centre console, gauge pod and side grille.
Metallic rings on heater controls.
260km/h speedometer.
Aluminium gearshift boot with limited-edition serial number. (Numbered plate also in engine bay.)
Special red hazard warning light switch.
Owner's manual with suede cover.
Leather key fob with limited-edition serial number.

Engine:
1994cc engine with 320bhp and 420Nm; hand-assembled.
Larger turbocharger with additional blades and ball-bearing turbine shaft.
Sports ECU.
Balanced pistons, con-rods and crankshaft.
High-flow catalytic converter.
High-flow silencer made from lightweight titanium, saving 5kg (11lb).
Oil cooler.
Long-life, flex-resistant, silicone connectors on intercooler and turbocharger air intake.

Running gear:
Ride height lowered by 15mm (0.6in).
Spring rates increased by 50 per cent.
Aluminium lateral suspension links with 'pillow-ball' bushes.
Larger-diameter rear anti-roll bar.
Ball-jointed rear anti-roll bar bracket.
DCCD.
Helical front LSD.
Mechanical rear LSD.
Four-way adjustable dampers.
Oil cooler for PAS.
Grooved brake discs.
Lightweight 18-inch BBS forged alloy wheels (6kg/13lb lighter than standard STI 17-inch types).
Pirelli P-Zero Corsa tyres.

S204 (2005)

600 Examples
The S204 edition was based on the WRX STI and was broadly similar to the S203. It was introduced in late 2005. Although most cars were for the Japanese market, some were also shipped abroad, for example to Singapore. Five cars exported to New Zealand did not have numbered limited-edition badges, but it is not clear if these were additional to the 600 that Subaru claims to have built.

Bodywork:
Special grille.
No roof spoiler.
Front lip spoiler made of carbon fibre.
Rear diffuser under bumper.

Interior:
Special Recaro seats with very high side bolsters.
Individually numbered limited-edition plaque at base of gear lever. (Numbered plate also in engine bay.)

Engine:
1994cc STI engine with 320PS (316bhp) and 318lb ft.
Standard STI six-speed gearbox.

Running gear:
High-performance dampers, branded with both STI and Yamaha logos.

WR-Limited (2005)

Unknown Total
The WR-Limited was a special edition based on the WRX saloon and announced in August 2005. It was issued to celebrate the inclusion of a Japanese round (30 September to 2 October) of the 2005 World Rally Championship.

Bodywork:
WR Blue Mica paint.
STI front air-dam extension.
Fog-light covers with SWRT decals.
HID headlights.
SWRT decals on front doors.
Special UV rear glass.
Tall rear spoiler with SWRT logo.
Special boot-lid emblem.

Interior:
Front seats trimmed in blue alcantara, with SWRT logos.
Blue carpets.
Blue alcantara-backed slip-case for vehicle handbooks.
Scale model of WRC car engine.

Engine:
1994cc WRX type.

Running gear:
Manual or automatic gearbox.
17-inch forged RAYS alloy wheels with gold finish.

WRX STI Spec C Type RA (2005)

350 Examples
Like the WR-Limited, this edition was announced in August 2005. It was based on the STI Spec C car.

Bodywork:
Premium Silver Metallic, Pure White, or WR Blue paint.
STI front air dam.
Special decals on doors.
Special boot lid emblem.
STI exhaust finisher.

Interior:
Alcantara front seat trim with STI logo.

Soft-touch black paint on dash.
Aluminium gear lever surround.
Automatic air conditioning.
Electric mirrors and windows.
Remote central locking.

Engine:
1994cc STI type.

Running gear:
Lowered suspension.
Adjustable dampers.
Alloy suspension links with 'pillow-ball' bushes.
Uprated rear anti-roll bar.
8Jx17 12-spoke STI wheels with silver-grey finish.

WRX STI Spec C V-Limited (2005)

Unknown Total
The V-Limited derivative of the Spec C cars was announced in autumn 2005 for the 2006 model-year. It carried decals for Team Arai, the Subaru-focused team run by Japanese driver Toshihiro Arai.

Bodywork:
STI front lip spoiler.
Fog-light covers with Subaru Team Arai logos.
Subaru Team Arai decals on doors.
'V-Limited' badge on boot lid.
Rear spoiler with Subaru Team Arai logos.

Interior:
Blue and black STI-style upholstery.
Gearknob with titanium finish.

Engine:
1994cc STI type.

Running gear:
Wheels finished in white.

WRX STI Spec C Type RA-R (2006)

300 Examples
This limited edition was introduced in late October 2006

and was based on the WRX STI Spec C models. The final 'R' in the designation supposedly stands for 'radical'.

Bodywork:
Blue, white or yellow paint.
RA-type lip spoiler.
Lightweight glass.
Thinner roof with RA-type roof spoiler.
Alloy boot lid.
Optional carbon-fibre rear wing spoiler.

Interior:
Rear crossbar to stiffen body shell.
Optional Recaro sports front seats.

Engine:
1994cc engine with 320PS (316bhp) and 318lb ft.
Engine blueprinted and balanced.
Turbocharger based on twin-scroll type used in S203 and S204 models.
Oil cooler.
Optional sports exhaust

Running gear:
Lowered suspension, incorporating STI tuning parts.
Optional stiffer springs.
Optional larger anti-roll bars.
Strut brace.
Six-piston Brembo front brakes.
Optional larger brakes.
Grooved brake discs that change from silver to gold when heated in use.
White-finish Enkei 18-inch alloy wheels with STI logos.
Optional silver-finish wheels.

AUSTRALIAN SPECIAL EDITIONS

WRX Club Spec Evo 5 (2002)

140 Saloons, 60 Sports Wagons
The run of Club Spec editions in Australia continued with the Club Spec Evo 5, introduced in February 2002. Even though automatic-transmission WRX models were available in Australia, the Evo 5 cars all had manual gearboxes.

Bodywork:
Orange paint.
Electric sunroof.
Special badges.

Interior:
High-specification ICE system.
Numbered limited-edition plate on centre console.

Engine:
1994cc.

Running gear:
As standard.

WRX Club Spec Evo 6 (2003)

200 Examples
The annual Club Spec edition for 2003 was introduced that April and followed a familiar format. All cars still had manual gearboxes.

Bodywork:
Graphite Black Mica, Premium Silver Metallic or WR Blue paint.
Electric sunroof.
Special badges.

Interior:
Leather upholstery.
Side airbags.
Numbered limited-edition plate on centre console.

Engine:
1994cc.

Running gear:
As standard.

WRX Club Spec Evo 7 (2004)

300 Examples
The 2004 edition of the annual Club Spec edition was announced in January and shown to the public at the Brisbane Motor Show in February 2004. This was the first Aus-tralian special edition on which automatic transmission was an option.

Bodywork:
Graphite Black Mica, Premium Silver Metallic or WR Blue paint.
Electric sunroof.
Special badges.

Interior:
Leather upholstery.
Side airbags.
Numbered limited-edition plate on centre console.

Engine:
1994cc.

Running gear:
Optional four-speed automatic gearbox.

Petter Solberg Edition (2004)

200 Examples
This limited edition was announced at the Melbourne Show in September 2004. Both manual and automatic gearboxes were available, and the cars cost the same as standard WRX models.

Bodywork:
WR Blue paint.

Interior:
Numbered limited-edition plate on centre console.
Special gear knob.
Special key ring and fob.

Engine:
1994cc.

Running gear:
Optional four-speed automatic gearbox.

WRX WRP 10 (2005)

200 Examples
The WRP10 became available in January 2005 and cost

$48,490 (AUS). It was exclusive to Australia and celebrated 10 years of Subaru's partnership with Pirelli tyres (which explains the 'P' and the '10' in the name). 'WR' referred to World Rally.

Bodywork:
Mesh grille.

Interior:
Sports front seats.
Leather-rim steering wheel.
Metallic finish on dash and centre console.
'Sports' pedals.
Six-speaker ICE system.
Climate Control air conditioning.
Driver and passenger airbags.
Cruise control.

Engine:
1994cc engine, with 235bhp at 6000rpm and 302Nm (223lb ft) at 4000rpm.
ECU modified by STI.
Modified exhaust system with large-bore single tailpipe.

Running gear:
Ride height lowered by 15mm (0.6in).
STI springs.
STI carbon-fibre engine bay strut brace.
Gunmetal-finish RAYS five-spoke monobloc forged alloy wheels, 7Jx17, with carbon centre cap bearing 'STI RAYS' logo.
Pirelli P Zero Nero 215/45ZR17 tyres.

WRX Club Spec Evo 8 (2005)

300 Examples
The Evo 8 edition was introduced in April 2005. Both manual and automatic gearboxes were available.

Bodywork:
Champagne or Crystal Grey paint.
Electric sunroof.
Special decal badges.

Interior:
Leather upholstery.
Side airbags.
Numbered limited-edition plate on centre console.

Engine:
1994cc.

Running gear:
Optional four-speed automatic gearbox.

WRX Club Spec Evo 9 (2006)

300 Examples
The Evo 8 edition was introduced in April 2005. Both manual and automatic gearboxes were available.

Bodywork:
Obsidian Black or WR Blue paint.
Front lip spoiler.
Electric sunroof.
Special decal badges.

Interior:
Leather upholstery.
Numbered limited-edition plate on centre console.
STI aluminium gear knob with manual gearbox.
Quickshift gear change with manual gearbox.

Engine:
1994cc.

Running gear:
Suspension lowered by 15mm (0.6in).
18-inch wheels and space-saver space.
Optional four-speed automatic gearbox.

CHAPTER 9

THE THIRD GENERATION

Just as there had been two body styles for the first- and second-generation Imprezas, so the third-generation or type GE car was developed. But this time, there was a difference. The five-door estate that had been known in some markets as the Sports Wagon had not been universally liked, and Subaru decided not to replace it directly. As a result, alongside the expected four-door Impreza saloon came a five-door hatchback as the second body style.

All this demonstrated that Subaru were taking careful note of what their rivals were doing. There had been an obvious trend in recent years towards increasingly powerful hatchback models aimed at the market niche traditionally occupied by the Impreza WRX. Having both saloon and hatchback styles available would put the company in the best position to follow the market trend if it stayed with hatchbacks, or to revert to saloons if that seemed more appropriate.

In the beginning, the company decided to focus on the hatchback as the performance model, with the result that WRX and WRX STI derivatives were all based on the five-door car and looked very different indeed from the cars they replaced. Impreza enthusiasts all round the world were both shocked and disappointed by this move.

In a logical development, the third-generation Impreza was no longer a completely stand-alone design. Instead, it was based on the platform of the larger Legacy, suitably shortened to give a wheelbase of 2625mm (103.3in), which was still 93mm (3.75in) longer than that of the outgoing car. Although the wheelbase was longer, the overall length of the car was actually less, owing to improved packaging. Among the other benefits was a larger boot, made possible by the more compact multi-link rear suspension of the Legacy platform. Up front, the suspension remained true to MacPherson struts.

The two body shells were of course designed specifically for the Impreza, and a great deal of work was done to minimize weight. Even though the third-generation Impreza was bigger, stiffer and more resistant to crash damage than earlier models, it was not significantly heavier. In one major change, the door windows in both models now had full frames, to reduce the wind noise at speed that had been so characteristic of the two earlier generations of Impreza. It was a change that also greatly helped refinement.

As before, there was a wide Impreza range, which started with a 1.5-litre engine and went on up to a 2.5-litre, with a naturally aspirated 2.0-litre type for family saloons. At this point, the cars for the Japanese domestic market (JDM) diverged markedly from those for most export territories. While export WRX and WRX STI models, including of course those for the UK, continued with the 2.5-litre engine, the JDM cars reverted to a further development of the 2.0-litre flat-four. The 2.5-litre engines had type number EJ257, came with single-scroll VF48 turbochargers, shared a number of components with the Legacy GT engine and in top STI tune came with 300PS at 6000rpm with peak torque of 407Nm (300lb ft) at 4000rpm. The Japanese-market 2.0-litre engines had type number EJ207 and were more powerful despite their smaller swept volume. They came with a twin-scroll turbocharger and delivered 308PS (304bhp) at 6400rpm and 422Nm (311lb ft) at 4400rpm.

For the high-performance WRX STI models and on versions of the WRX exported to some territories, Subaru standardized its multi-mode VDC (Vehicle Dynamics Control) traction control system. This had 'Normal', 'Traction' and 'Off' settings. The familiar DCCD (Driver Controlled Centre Differential) was also standard, with four different settings to vary the front-to-rear torque bias.

The trouble was, it did not look like an Impreza ... the third-generation WRX arrived in the UK as a five-door hatchback, and even the WR Blue colour scheme on this example couldn't make it look like the Imprezas that enthusiasts were used to. A toned-down exhaust burble didn't help much, either.

GE Models, 2008 on

Engine (Japanese specification 2.0-litre)

Subaru EJ20 horizontally opposed four-cylinder. Aluminium block and heads; twin-scroll turbocharger with air-cooled intercooler; various different types of turbocharger were used for different variants.

Capacity	1994cc
Bore and stroke	92 x 75mm
Compression ratio	Varies for different types and models
Fuel system	Multi-point injection
Valve gear	Four overhead camshafts (two on each cylinder bank); four valves per cylinder

308PS at 6400rpm and 311lb ft at 4400rpm (WRX models)
300PS at 6200rpm and 258lb ft from 3000-6000rpm (A-line models)

Engine (Export-specification 2.5-litre)

Subaru EJ25 horizontally opposed four-cylinder. Aluminium block and heads; turbocharger with air-cooled intercooler; various different types of turbocharger were used for different variants.

Capacity	2457cc
Bore and stroke	99.5 x 79mm
Compression ratio	Varies for different types and models
Fuel system	Multi-point injection
Valve gear	Four overhead camshafts (two on each cylinder bank); four valves per cylinder; ACVS (Active Valve Control System)

230PS at 5200rpm and 236lb ft at 2800rpm (WRX models)
300PS at 6000rpm and 300lb ft at 4000rpm (WRX STI models)

Gearbox

Six-speed manual with overdrive fifth and sixth gears. Five-speed automatic with overdrive fifth gear available in some countries.

Final drive gearing
3.75:1 (WRX)
3.9:1 (WRX STI)
3.58:1 (automatic)

Steering

Power-assisted rack and pinion, speed-sensitive.

Suspension

Front: MacPherson struts with coil springs, L-shaped transverse link, and anti-roll bar.
Rear: Multi-link type with double wishbones, coil springs and anti-roll bar.

Brakes

Anti-Lock Brakes (ABS) with Electronic Brake-Force Distribution (EBD) and brake assist; Hill Holder system. Ventilated discs all round, with twin-piston calipers at the front and sliding calipers at the rear.

Weights and measures

Wheelbase	2625mm (103.3in)
Front track	1529mm (60.2in)
Rear track	1539mm (60.6in)
Length	4415mm (173.8in)
Width	1795mm (70.7in)
Height	1475mm (58.1in)
Wheels	17in or 18in according to model
Tyres	Varies according to model; see text
Unladen weight	1505–1539kg (3317–3395lb), depending on model. For wide-body cars, add 15kg (33lb).

It was very noticeable now how much importance Subaru attached to the US market. In fact, the 2008 model WRX was announced at the New York Auto Show in April 2007, some months before it was announced for other markets. In days gone by, US customers would probably have had to wait until the shows early in the next year before they got to see a new car, but Subaru chose to get this one into the USA as quickly as possible. The early introduction fuelled sales for the 2008 model-year, which, in the USA, started in the summer of 2007.

THE 2008 MODELS

European-market derivatives of the third-generation Impreza made their appearance at the Frankfurt Show in September 2007. That same show also saw the public debut of the 2008 WRC Impreza, of which pictures had been circulated to the media in August. Strictly speaking, the car was still a 'concept' at that stage, but what was most striking to Impreza enthusiasts was that the 2008 WRC car was to be based on the new hatchback body. The official explanation for this was that the hatchback's shorter overhangs made it better suited to rally work than the companion saloon.

For the UK, the basic WRX hatchback had a 2.5-litre turbocharged engine with 230bhp at 5200rpm and 236lb

ft at 2800rpm. Both maxima were generated much further down the rev range than before. The 0–60mph time was a very respectable 5.5 seconds – fast, but not the fastest Impreza yet. But there were disappointments, including the fact that the characteristic exhaust burble of the flat-four engine had been toned right down to the point at which it was almost non-existent. Refinement was all very well, but this was not what fans of the high-performance Imprezas wanted at all. The interior was also disappointing, although perhaps Impreza enthusiasts should have expected the large expanses of hard and shiny plastic that had become almost a Subaru trademark. The steering wheel, at least, had a thick rim with leather trim.

The WRC car was based on the STI derivative of the third-generation car, and this was introduced to the public at the Tokyo Show in October 2007. It turned out to be a wide-body derivative of the hatchback, thus ending all hopes within the enthusiast fraternity that there might in the short term be a new WRX Impreza that at least looked something like the much-loved earlier models. The widened wings added 56mm (2.2in) to the overall width of the car, and of course made room for wider wheels and tyres.

For the UK market, the STI derivative was known as a WRX STI Type UK and cost £24,995, which was some £1600 less than the second-generation car it replaced. A number of inlet and exhaust components were shared with the Legacy

It was business as usual in the WRX's cabin, with acres of grey plastic, even though the whole interior had been redersigned for the new car.

GT version of the engine, and there was a larger intercooler than before, although this time without the red STI lettering that had distinguished previous generations of the car. ACVS variable valve timing was also incorporated. The STI engine had 300PS (296bhp) at 6000rpm and 300lb ft of torque at 4000rpm. Acceleration was certainly impressive, and the car could reach 60mph from standstill in 4.8 seconds.

The new WRX STI came with a six-speed gearbox, Driver Controlled Centre Differential, and limited-slip differentials front and rear as standard. There were aluminium components in the suspension to reduce unsprung weight, and a new SI-Drive (Subaru Intelligent Drive) adjustable throttle mapping feature gave three modes, called Intelligent, Sport and Sport Sharp. Sports seats were standard equipment, with leather and alcantara upholstery.

When *Autocar* tried out a WRX STI Type UK in its issue of 5 March 2008, it could not hide a tone of disappointment. In an earlier test (of the 2.0RS hatchback model, dated 10 October 2007), the magazine had already made its overall views on the third-generation car plain: 'There is a lot to like about the new Impreza, but it feels like a job half done. Subaru's intention to create a car capable of appealing to the mainstream market is commendable, but only the WRX and STI versions kept the previous generation alive in a marketplace that has long since turned away from non-premium saloons.

> *The family hatch has moved on while Subaru has been developing the Impreza and it feels like it has been optimized against last-generation rivals. There are enough cheap-feeling materials to deny it the quality interior that buyers now demand.'*

The WRX STI was no thing of beauty, and once again the interior let it down. As *Autocar* put it,

> *... plenty of superminis costing half the money have cabins that are more appealingly styled, fabricated and finished than this. But it's an improvement, and if the sculpture of the main dashboard moulding looks a little odd, it has more substance about it than that of the previous car.*

Performance was certainly there for the taking, even though the magazine failed to equal the manufacturer's claimed 0–60mph time of 4.8 seconds and recorded only a best of 5.2 seconds. 'The flat four's responses are languid and this, coupled with the need to wind the turbo up, makes the STI feel slightly lazy. But thoughts of slothfulness are banished when you opt for "sport sharp" and mash the throttle. Beyond 4000rpm the engine is pulling with such urgency that you'll need a hand on the gear lever in readiness for the rev limit's 6700rpm arrival. If you're too slow, you'll hit a slightly savage limiter.'

Ultimately, it was this disappointing off-boost performance and sudden transition to urgent acceleration that counted against the car. 'This near-instant change of personality makes the STI feel slightly unwilling at an ambling-to-brisk pace, but almost manic with enthusiasm if you're feeling the same way…hardcore enthusiasts will be disappointed by a dynamic personality that is almost bipolar, the shift between its languid mid-speed pace and its press-on dynamism too great to make it a thrilling car for enough of the time.' Fuel consumption, too, was a major disappointment, with a miserable overall figure of 15.6 l/100km (18.1mpg).

The WRX STI was also based on the new hatchback body. These are RHD examples but for the Japanese market. UK-spec cars did not have the bumper-mounted fog lights.

RIGHT AND BELOW: *The name of the 2010-model Impreza WRX STI Type UK was a mouthful, and it offered plenty of performance, but it was still based on the hatchback shell. By this stage, enthusiasts knew that Subaru UK had to do something, and quickly.*

The under-bonnet view of the WRX STI Type UK was generally familiar, but the STI models no longer had an STI logo emblazoned across the intercooler. The engine was of course the 2.5-litre type; Japanese cars had a slightly more powerful 2.0-litre.

The wide-body STI Type UK had these front wings with air outlets and STI logos. Note also the black-painted brake clipper with an STI logo, and the STI logo repeated on the rim of the 10-spoke alloy wheel.

The WRX STI Type UK fortunately carried simplified badging: at the rear, it just read 'STI Impreza'.

Red-lit dials were an STI characteristic, and pink STI logos here and there helped to lift the greyness of the interior a little. Note also the drilled alloy pedals. SI-Drive allowed the driver to tune the engine's responses, and the control below it was for the Driver Controlled Centre Differential.

2009 MODEL-YEAR: LOST ENTHUSIASM

The disappointing reception for the new 2008 models got the third-generation Imprezas off to a bad start among performance enthusiasts. And things were to get worse as the year wore on.

In the mean time, the company had been doing some fast footwork to improve the appeal of the WRX and WRX STI models in the UK, and for the 2009 model-year that began in the autumn of 2008, it had called on the services of Prodrive, who came up with a tempting array of special-edition cars. These were announced early, at the British International Motor Show held at London's ExCel Centre in July 2008, and there were no fewer than three of them. At that stage, all were tipped for availability by the end of the year, although in practice only two did become production models, with the first deliveries beginning in September.

At the bottom of the pecking order came the £22,495 WRX-S, based on the standard-body WRX hatchback. Changes to the ECU and a modified exhaust system improved the power to 255PS at 5400rpm and the torque to 288lb ft at 3000rpm, reducing the 0–60mph acceleration to 5.5 seconds.

Next up was the WRX STI 330S which, as its name suggested, was based on the wide-body WRX STI. Curiously, this model was announced but not actually displayed at the ExCel show. The Prodrive modifications to the car took engine power up to 330PS (325bhp), which of course provided the name. That peak power was generated at 5400rpm, while maximum torque of 467Nm (347lb ft) was reached at 3400rpm. Both figures were achieved significantly lower in the rev range than on the standard STI engine, and the result was a 0–60mph time of 4.4 seconds, which was real giant-killing performance.

One specific aim of the 330S was to compete with the UK-specification Mitsubishi Lancer Evolution X FQ-330, and the car was priced at £30,000, but Subaru were also aware that an indefinable something was missing from the GE models. The 330S therefore had a special exhaust system with 90-mm (3.6-in) stainless-steel pipes that was claimed to restore the burbling noise that was so much a part of the Impreza tradition. Recaro bucket front seats, leather upholstery, a satellite navigation system, a 'keyless go' ignition system and 8.5Jx18-inch five-spoke alloy

wheels were all part of the standard specification. The car was made available in the full range of STI colours; for further details, see Chapter 11.

Right at the top was the WRX STI 380S, officially a concept but for some time tipped as a production reality by insiders at Subaru. However, on 10 September 2008, Subaru UK announced that this model would not go into production, because of unspecified 'homologation and specification problems'. That was probably code for the fact that it would not meet emissions regulations and could not be produced at a realistic price. It was a shame: the 380S would probably have been built as a limited-production model and featured a number of Prodrive enhancements including a new body kit and an extensively reworked engine and special exhaust, which between them achieved the 380PS (375bhp) that gave the car its name. The show car wore 8.5Jx18-inch BBS alloys, which were expected to be available in silver or gold, and the tyres were 245/40R18s all round.

Auto Express tried a 330S in November 2008, and reported that 'in true Impreza style, the power arrives with a thump once the turbo comes on boost – quite unlike the more linear delivery in its Mitsubishi Evo X rival…But it's the savage crescendo as the engine builds towards the 8000rpm red line that really gives this car its character.' The steering, though, was criticized for being too light and failing to provide enough feedback. Evo magazine had a similar reaction when it tried a car in January 2009: 'the steering – particularly in the crucial fractions of a second when you turn into a corner – was as disconcertingly light and devoid of feel as that of any other current Impreza.' Writer Peter Tomalin's conclusion was not a positive one: 'I couldn't really recommend the "S" over the regular STI, which gives you virtually the same bang for considerably less buck. And Scooby fans everywhere are still waiting for the Impreza to rediscover the magic we all know lurks somewhere within.' Something was evidently still missing.

At the end of 2008, there was news from Subaru that was to have an even greater impact on the new Impreza than the negative reviews. Enthusiasts' hopes for the success of the new car on the world rally scene were dashed when, on 16 December, the company announced that it was withdrawing from the WRC for reasons associated with the recent major downturn in the world economic situation. Rallying is an expensive business, even if it brings huge rewards in terms of publicity, and Subaru was not alone in looking to cut costs. Fellow Japanese competitor Suzuki had made a similar announcement just one day earlier, and symptomatic of the same concern for the future was Land Rover's decision to cancel its world-wide G4 Challenge event two days later, on 18 December. None the less, it must have been a difficult decision for Subaru to make, and it certainly did nothing to increase enthusiast interest in the latest Impreza models.

2010 MODELS: BEGINNING THE LONG HAUL BACK

Car sales in the UK were in the doldrums in the early part of 2009, as manufacturers scratched around to find something that would tempt buyers into the showrooms at a time when the economic situation looked extremely gloomy. This was not the time to spend money on improved specifications, and Subaru did not; the 2010 models that arrived in autumn 2009 were distinguished by nothing more exciting than a minor facelift from a new grille insert. But there was hope on the horizon, even if at Motor Show time nobody was talking about plans for the future.

With the end of Subaru's WRC challenge in 2008, Prodrive gradually faded from the picture, and quickly forged links with other manufacturers. Subaru UK decided to turn to another leading UK performance consultancy to develop a new high-performance Impreza that would attract attention to the marque and retain interest. It had to be something exceptional in its own right, because there was now no factory involvement in the WRC to provide favourable publicity for the Impreza. In a word, Subaru were looking for what is usually called a 'halo product'.

The consultancy they turned to was Cosworth and the result was the Cosworth Impreza CS400. The new model was announced in May 2010, priced at an astronomically high £49,995 (with even a WRX STI costing no more than £27,590), and limited to just 75 cars – unsurprisingly, demand was not expected to be high. Some examples were still in stock more than a year after the launch.

The Cosworth Impreza was just the first part of a determined effort by Subaru to win back performance enthusiasts who had become disenchanted with the marque after the disappointment of the hatchback third-generation performance models and the 2008 withdrawal from the World Rally Championship. But it would be a long, hard haul back from that low point.

Cosworth

Cosworth Engineering was named after its founders, Mike Costin and Keith Duckworth. It made its name in Formula 1 racing in the 1960s, but subsequently broadened its business to include engineering consultancy for a wider customer base. Its name has always been associated with high performance, and in particular with engines. An association with Ford in Britain produced the legendary Ford Cosworth DFV 3-litre racing engine, which from 1967 had a career lasting more than 20 years and became the most successful Formula 1 engine ever.

From 1969, Cosworth developed a number of road engines for Ford, in particular the BDA family. From the mid-1980s there were other legendary high-performance Fords such as the Sierra RS Cosworth and later the Escort RS Cosworth. From 1990, the company belonged to Vickers plc, and from 1998 the racing division belonged to Ford while the engineering division became Cosworth Technology and was sold to the VW-Audi Group. Cosworth Technology was sold to Mahle in 2005 and became Mahle Powertrain.

The new CS400 was clearly a big-budget operation, and Cosworth had spared no costs in redeveloping the 2.5-litre engine to produce a massive 400PS. The company claimed that the new car would hit 60mph from rest in a quite astonishing 3.7 seconds. Uprated suspension and front brakes added to the car's performance credentials; there was a tougher single-plate clutch; and the top three gear ratios had been modified with carbon synchromesh to cope with the extra torque. For fuller details of the car's specification, see Chapter 11.

Impressive though the Cosworth car undoubtedly was, it did not please everybody. *Evo* magazine on the web in June 2010 complained that, 'the trouble is the extensive modifications haven't resulted in a stunning driving experience. The flat four is surprisingly laggy with boost arriving in a rush after 3500rpm. From there on it's mightily rapid, and consumes each of its gears very quickly. Too quickly. Longer gearing would have helped matters.' Other commentators also singled out the turbocharger lag as one of the car's negative features.

Evo magazine would have welcomed weightier steering, too: 'As it stands it's too light and wayward around the straight-ahead, meaning the CS400 doesn't move into the first part of a corner with anything like the determination and energy it should. There's even a little understeer. Until you get back on the power, where the 4wd struts its stuff, order is restored, traction is found and the Impreza does what it does best – gets out of the corner in a jiffy, gasping for the next gear.'

2011: SOMETHING RADICAL

Subaru's announcements in October 2010 for the 2011 model-year had an effect not unlike a pair of grenades going off. First, the high-performance Impreza models were no longer going to be called Imprezas in the UK; that name would be reserved for the lesser models of the range and the high-performance cars would now be known as the Subaru WRX and Subaru WRX STI. Second, those high-performance models would now be available not only with the hatchback body style but optionally with the latest four-door saloon style. At last, it seemed, enthusiasts would be able to buy something new that had visual links to the WRX models of old.

The WRX STI was quite extensively overhauled in an attempt to win back the enthusiast market, and most

noticeably the handling was tightened up by using the Japanese-market 'Spec C' or competition-oriented suspension set-up. This meant rear springs that were an astonishing 53 per cent stiffer than before, front springs 15 per cent stiffer than on the 2010 cars, uprated anti-roll bars both front and rear, plus a ride height lowered by 15mm (0.6mm). The wheels were now 18-inch alloys and each one was 2kg (4.5lb) lighter than earlier types, reducing unsprung mass to compensate for the stiffer suspension and give a better ride. Subaru also claimed to have reinforced the body shell to cope with the harder suspension.

The car had been facelifted, too, with new and more aggressive bumpers, some minor changes to the rear panels, and (on the four-door saloon) a boot-lid spoiler. However, this was a spoiler that was both optional and discreet, and not at all like the large wings of the classic Imprezas; nor, curiously, was it the tall rear wing spoiler available in some other markets. There was more bad news from the colour options list, where the classic WR Blue was no longer to be found. Inside, Subaru claimed improvements in the quality of cabin fittings, but these were still not as classy as those offered by most of the car's obvious rivals.

However, the really good news was that, as *Top Gear* magazine put it, 'the burble is very definitely back'. Even though the engine was in the same state of tune as before, with 300PS and 300lb ft of torque, there had obviously been some re-tuning of the exhaust system. The distinctive

At last! For 2011, Subaru brought the four-door saloon back into the STI range. It was never going to be an attractive car, but at least it looked like the hot Imprezas that enthusiasts had worshipped for close on 20 years.

By 2011, it was time to rebuild the turbocharged Impreza's image. A record lap of the Isle of Man TT course by former British Rally Champion Mark Higgins certainly did it no harm.

As part of Subaru UK's publicity offensive to re-establish the high-performance Impreza models in the market-place, a Cosworth CS400 challenged for honours at the 2011 Cholmondeley Pageant of Power.

Racing in Europe was also helping to rebuild the hot Impreza's tarnished image. This WRX STI tS claimed SP3T class honours at the Nürburgring 24-hour race in June 2011. Drivers were Toshihiro Yoshida and Kouta Sasaki.

sound of the turbocharged flat-four engine was now plain for all to hear once again. As always, there was massive mid-range punch from the engine, spoiled only by the relatively poor off-boost performance. The driving experience had been improved by those suspension revisions, too. On the road, the 2011-model WRX STI felt much stiffer than its third-generation predecessors, and although the ride was a little unsettling over some surfaces, the steering feel was good and the body control excellent.

One major problem did blight this catalogue of mostly good news, however. The Japanese Yen had strengthened considerably against the pound, and the UK importers had no choice but to increase the price by very nearly 20 per cent, so that the WRX STI now cost £32,995. This put it on a level with some much more sophisticated machinery, and as a result the car was in danger of losing its appeal as a bargain-basement high-performance saloon.

But Subaru's determination to win back performance enthusiasts did not end there. By the spring of 2011, it was offering a power upgrade to 320PS and a satellite navigation system for no additional cost. Then, towards the middle of the year, it hired former British Rally champion Mark Higgins to demonstrate the performance of its latest cars as publicly as possible. So in June, Higgins took a WRX STI saloon to the Isle of Man for an attempt to break the road-car lap record for the TT circuit. The record run was made during the TT event, and in order to fit it in to the race's busy schedule, the Subaru team were allowed just one circuit of the course and no warm-up or practice laps.

The previous record had been set 21 years ago to the day, on 6 June 1990, by Tony Pond in a Rover 827 Vitesse. The Subaru was in theory a perfectly standard car, but it did incorporate some essential modifications. The springs and dampers had been adjusted to minimize damage over the course's high-speed bumps and jumps, and the car had an MSA-specification T45 integrated roll cage, TRS race harnesses and a Lifeline extinguisher system.

The attempt was successful, knocking more than two minutes off the existing lap record. It was 'both the most exhilarating and the most frightening thing I have ever done', Mark Higgins said afterwards. 'The rules allow for a flying start, so I crossed the line at 125mph [200km/h]. I then went down through the Bray Hill junction – normally taken at around 20mph [32km/h] – at over 150mph [240km/h]. Once that tricky section was out of the way I settled into the lap and quickly got used to the balance and sheer pace of the car.

In the end the lap was simply fantastic, and the WRX STI behaved impeccably. That we managed to set such an impressive time at our first attempt is a great tribute to the Subaru, especially given that so few modifications have been made. The engine pulled incredibly strongly throughout and the cornering capability proved crucial on such a twisty, unforgiving course.

Higgins also reported that the TT crowds got fully behind the record attempt. 'The atmosphere out on the circuit was incredible,' he said, 'especially once the spectators heard over the PA system that we were in the process of setting a new record. I could hear the cheers in the car and it really added to the experience.'

In July, the Subaru name was once again thrust under the nose of media and public when Higgins put on an electrifying display with the Cosworth CS400 at the Cholmondely Pageant of Power. In the final standings, it finished second only to a £186,000 Lamborghini LP570-4 Performante. Higgins' best time on the twisty 1.9-km (1.2-mile) sprint circuit was 66.08 seconds, at an average speed of 105.33km/h (65.45mph). Subaru UK jubilantly claimed that the result established the Cosworth as the fastest hot hatch in the 'supercar' class.

2012 MY: LAST OF THE OLD MODELS

There were only small changes for the 2012 model-year, including bright headlamp backing panels instead of the black ones on earlier cars. The boot trim on the four-doors was now body-coloured instead of satin-finish, and the centre console panel switched to grey from the silver (Plasma Blue Pearl) on earlier cars.

By the end of 2011, Subaru had also confirmed that the next-generation WRX, which was due in mid-2012 as a 2013 model, would have a turbocharged version of the new FA-type direct-injection, 2.0-litre flat-four that had already been announced for the BRZ sports car that became available early in 2012. A redesigned Impreza had already made its appearance as a 2012 model in some markets, riding on a longer wheelbase and featuring a more steeply angled windscreen and more interior space. However, Subaru's plan was to build the new WRX and WRX STI models on a platform of their own rather than as derivatives of the Impreza range.

THE IMPREZA WRX GE
IN OTHER MARKETS

Subaru continued to build cars to suit market conditions in different groups of countries worldwide.

Japanese-Spec Cars

From the start of GE-series production, the WRX and WRX STI cars for the Japanese domestic market had a different engine from the one used for most export markets. This was the latest version of the 2.0-litre EJ207 type, half a litre smaller than the export EJ257 engine but no less powerful thanks to the use of a twin-scroll turbocharger instead of the export-specification single-scroll type.

The 2009 model-year started without major change for the WRX and WRX STI ranges, although in early October 2008 Impreza enthusiasts were attracted by the Subaru Takumi concept that was shown at the Motor Sport Japan show in Tokyo. However, rumours that it was the much-anticipated Spec or competition-biased model proved unfounded, and the car was later confirmed to be an early look at the 20th Anniversary Edition WRX STI due for 2009 release.

There was, however, an important new model early in the 2009 calendar year. This was the WRX STI A-line, announced on 24 February and combining STI performance – or at least, most of it – with an automatic gearbox. It was that gearbox that gave the new model its name. The A-Line was another step in the direction pioneered by cars such as the UK-market Spec D. It offered as much as possible of the WRX STI performance but without the brash, youth-oriented appeal. Large spoilers and red brake calipers were out.

To retain performance with the five-speed automatic gearbox, Subaru fitted the A-line cars with the 2.5-litre engine, equipped with dual ACVS and a single-scroll turbocharger. The engine had 300PS at 6200rpm and peak torque of 350Nm (258lb ft) generated between 3000 and 6000rpm, while the gearbox had Sportshift paddle controls on the steering wheel (designed in the UK by Prodrive). It also had the oddly named Downshifting Blipping Control. This simply described what happened when the transmission shifted down a gear: electronic communica-

tion between engine and gearbox raised the engine revs slightly to ensure the downchange was a smooth one. The A-line car was available only in Japan and Singapore when launched, but was later sold also in Hong Kong, and from July 2010 in Indonesia. Australian deliveries also began in 2011. Even though the car was lighter than a manual-gearbox WRX STI, at 1490kg (3278lb) compared with 1505kg (3311lb), its acceleration was slower and the 0–60mph sprint took 6.1 seconds.

Even though the 2009 A-line was deliberately toned down, it retained just enough of the STI heritage to indicate to onlookers what it was. So although the Enkei wheels were titanium-coloured with black-painted Brembo brake calipers visible behind them, there was a black STI front lip. Inside, the creature comforts began with eight-way electric adjustment for the driver's seat. The leather upholstery option also brought front-seat heaters. The A-Line came with a new body colour of Satin White Pearl, which was probably deliberately intended to appeal to the traditional Japanese love of white. It sold well enough to remain in the line-up right through into the 2012 model-year.

Meanwhile, if Subaru had given up on the World Rally Championship, they had not thrown in the towel completely. In order to keep the WRX STI homologated for Group N events, they needed a stripped-out high-performance model. That arrived in July 2009 as the limited-volume WRX STI Spec C (for more details, see Chapter 11). Nor had the company forgotten the value of special editions. So at the start of 2010, Japanese showrooms began to display the R205 special edition, a top-performance model that followed in the sequence after the S204 model that had been based on the second-generation Impreza. That was followed in autumn 2011 by the S206, which reverted to the earlier prefix. For further details about both of these models, see Chapter 11.

For 2012, there was also a new variant of the A-line range, called the A-line Type S and available as either hatchback or saloon. While the basic A-line remained available, the Type S had a slightly harder edge, with a new rear spoiler, Recaro bucket seats in front, and a new style of 18-inch wheel. Still badged with the full name of Impreza WRX STI A-line Type S, it was likely to be one of the last new models from Subaru to combine the Impreza name with those six world-renowned initial letters.

North American-Spec Cars

The first US-specification WRX cars had the EJ 255 2.5-litre engine with Mitsubishi TD04 turbocharger and 230PS (227bhp), and were available with either five-speed manual or four-speed automatic gearboxes. They were coded GH. Automatic cars were heavier, at 1455kg (3208lb) as compared to 1425kg (3142lb) for the manuals. The cars no longer had four-piston front and two-piston rear brakes with fixed calipers, but instead had twin-piston fronts and single-piston rears with sliding calipers. The front brakes were now 295mm (11.6in) in diameter and the rears 287mm (11.3in).

The cars had 60/40 split folding rear seats as standard, and could be ordered with a Premium package which brought front bucket seats with two-stage heating. Also in the Premium package was a 100-watt, 10-speaker ICE system with an in-dash six-CD changer and satellite radio capability. The standard ICE system was an 80-watt type with six speakers and a single-disc CD player. There were auxiliary inputs for portable multimedia devices, and a touch-screen GPS navigation system was a further option (although this was not available on cars for Canada).
The WRX STI had 309PS (305bhp) and 390Nm (290lb ft) and had model code GR because of its wide-body styling, which added 56mm (1.9in) to the overall width. The cars weighed between 1505kg and 1540kg (3318–3395lb), depending on how many options were fitted.

As had been the case in other markets, customer criticism of the 2008 models suggested that they were too soft, so the 2009 US models had uprated engines with an IHI VF52 turbocharger and 269PS (265bhp) and 331Nm (244lb ft). The 0–60mph standing-start time was now 4.7 seconds. Automatic-transmission models were dropped (but were directly replaced by an Impreza 2.5 GT model, which used the engine and gearbox from the 2008 WRX). In Canada, the 269PS engine was an option only, on models called WRX 265 (the name reflecting the 265bhp rating).

The suspension was also uprated, with stiffer components taken from the STI models, and Dunlop SP Sport 01 summer performance tyres became standard equipment. An aerodynamic package was made standard, along with a new mesh grille with WRX badge and darker-coloured wheels.

The North American car market generally had a bad time during the economic recession of 2009, but Subaru actually increased its market share. So for 2010 there were no major changes, except that the 269PS 2.5-litre engine was standardized for Canada, and the 227bhp engine was discontinued.

For 2011, North American cars retained their Impreza name, and now came with a servicing requirement to use synthetic engine oil. As in other markets, there was concern that the WRX and WRX STI models were losing their appeal to younger buyers, so the WRX was given the wide-body styling and 38mm (1.5in) wider tracks of the WRX STI, with wider 8Jx17-inch wheels and 235/45R17 tyres. It also gained a pair of twin-exit exhausts and a rear diffuser. Inevitably, weight increased (by 33lb).

Meanwhile, the STI for North America was now available as both hatchback and four-door saloon with the wide-body style featuring flared wings, front skirts and rear valance. The saloon had a large wing spoiler at the rear recalling the classic hot Imprezas of earlier years. Suspension improvements included stiffer springs, bigger anti-roll bars and new 'pillow-ball' bushes on the lower front arms. The STI was claimed to run the 0–60mph sprint in 4.9 seconds.

The 2012 models for North America were announced at the New York Auto Show on 20 April 2011, but by that stage the actual arrival date in dealerships had already been put back to November. The Japanese earthquake and tsunami in March had led to production hold-ups at almost every one of the country's motor manufacturers.

This time, North American marketing fell into line with that in other markets, and the Impreza name was dropped for the high-performance derivatives. These were now marketed as Subaru WRX and WRX STI types. Both were available as four-door saloons and five-door hatchbacks; there were Premium and Limited option packages for the WRX models, and a Limited option pack for the four-door WRX STI.

The WRX models had 17-inch alloy wheels in gunmetal finish, with 15 spokes arranged in five groups of three. The STI saloon models had wheels with five split spokes, but there were 18-inch BBS alloys with nine sets of paired spokes for the five-door STI and as part of the Limited option package on the saloon. The STI also now had an adjustable rev counter alarm to prevent over-revving.

Australian-Spec Cars

Subaru Australia promoted the 2008 models with enthusiasm, and the company's Managing Director, Nick Senior, was certainly bullish in his approach: 'This is the car that

Subaru UK issued this picture of an 'Impreza Design Concept' in July 2011. Elsewhere, the fourth-generation model had already been revealed – but not yet in WRX or WRX STI form.

forever will re-define and shape the small car class. This is the car that tells all competitors: don't come to the table unless you tick all these boxes.' There was also a notice-able shift in the marketing, as Senior explained: 'WRX retains its award-winning performance credentials but delivers them through a far more mature and sophisticat-ed premium package that we are convinced will broaden its appeal. An increasing majority of new WRX buyers are professional people seeking a car that combines a degree of subtle style with an outstanding chassis and engine package.'

Only hatchback models were available at the start, the WRX with 2.5-litre engine and 230PS (227bhp) with 320Nm, and only with a five-speed manual gearbox. The Australian WRX was claimed to be good for 0–60mph times of 5.8 seconds. There were 17-inch alloy wheels as standard.

Despite the apparent confidence of the Managing Direc-tor, the reaction of the Australian customers was the same as in other markets – they were not happy. Within three months of the new cars going on sale, Subaru Australia real-ized that the GE-series car was alienating traditional WRX buyers. 'They wanted a WRX that was more in keeping with their expectations and what they had tasted over the years,' admitted a press release. Hatchback WRX STI models arrived early in 2008 to keep the pot boiling, and when the 2009 models appeared in September 2008, they cost the same but had more powerful engines, stiffened suspension supposedly developed specifically for Australia, and new tyres. Saloon models became available on lesser Imprezas at the same time, but there were no WRX saloons until December 2008, and no WRX STI saloons until late 2010.

For 2011, Australia retained the Impreza name for the WRX and WRX STI models. Both saloon and hatchback

By 2012, the Australian market had the full complement of WRX and WRX STI variants, in both body styles. Even so, the angle of this publicity photograph tends to suggest that the saloon body style was being played down.

models were available in STI guise, and there was also a luxury model called the WRX STI Spec R. Manual and automatic gearboxes were available, and Recaro sports seats were optional. The Spec R model came as standard with leather upholstery, a satellite navigation system and BBS alloy wheels. As elsewhere, the 2011 STI models had a new design of front bumper; engine power remained at 300PS (305bhp) with torque of 407Nm (300lb ft). The 2012 models came as saloon or hatchback, with Premium derivatives of the WRX and Spec R derivatives of the WRX STI.

...AND ON TO A FOURTH GENERATION

Subaru announced its fourth-generation Impreza models at the New York Show on 20 April 2011, the same event

where it introduced the 2012-model WRX and WRX STI for the USA. In Japan, the new models went on sale from 30 November 2011. However, the plan for all markets was to introduce WRX and WRX STI derivatives on the new platform later and, as noted above, to dissociate them from the Impreza name.

The new models again consisted of hatchback and saloon alternatives, and were coded as GJ and GP. They shared a wheelbase of 2644mm (104in), making them slightly more roomy than the outgoing third-generation cars. Subaru numbered light weight among their major advances, plus a new light-alloy boxer engine called the FB20 in 2.0-litre form. With this came either a five-speed manual gearbox or a continuously variable transmission, branded as Lineartronic.

So the WRX and WRX STI story will continue, some 20 years after it first began....

CHAPTER 10

THE RALLYING STORY, 2008

Sadly, the 2008 WRC Impreza was the last of its breed, but the fact that Subaru went to so much trouble to develop it at all underpins the company's commitment to the WRC event. It also lends credibility to the reasons they gave for withdrawal at the end of 2008. The first pictures of the car – officially a concept at that stage – were released to the media in August 2007, and serious testing began in December that year. Subaru's test driver this season was Märkko Martin, an Estonian driver who had driven for the Ford WRC team, later moving to Peugeot. In 2006, he had also driven a Group N Impreza at the Rally of Portugal.

The car was prepared, as usual, by Prodrive in the UK. It was based on the hatchback model, supposedly because this had shorter overhangs than the four-door saloon and therefore a lower polar moment of inertia (which essentially means it was less likely to spin in extreme conditions). Prodrive were singularly unimpressed by the new

What Were They Called?

Subaru identified its third-generation Impreza WRC cars as WRC2008 models. Prodrive meanwhile knew them as S14 types.

double-wishbone rear suspension, and converted it to the strut type used on the earlier, classic Imprezas.

Drivers Petter Solberg and Chris Atkinson had their first taste of the WRC2008 car during a four-day test in Sardinia between 30 April and 3 May 2008. The car scored a podium finish in its first event, when Solberg claimed second place in the Acropolis Rally that began on 29 May that year.

THIS PAGE AND OPPOSITE: *Subaru lost no time in showing a 'concept' version of the 2008 WRC car. The livery was not quite the way it would appear when the cars were used in anger.*

By the time the WRC2008 car proper was presented, there had been a number of changes from the concept. The rear spoiler was very different, and the side decals had changed. There were, of course, more sponsors' decals as well.

2008 SEASON

Events
Monte Carlo, 24–27 January
Sweden, 8–10 February
Mexico, 28 February–2 March
Argentina, 27–30 March
Jordan, 24–27 April
Sardinia, 16–18 May
Acropolis (Greece), 29 May–1 June
Turkey, 13–15 June
Finland, 31 July–3 August
Rallye Deutschland (Germany), 15–17 August
New Zealand, 28–31 August
Catalunya (Spain), 2–5 October
Tour de Corse (Corsica), 10–12 October
Japan, 31 October–2 November
RAC (Wales Rally GB), 5–7 December

Drivers
Petter Solberg/Phil Mills
Chris Atkinson/Stéphane Prévot
Brice Tirabassi/Fabrice Gordon

Cars

1 WRC	C1 WRC
2 WRC	and others
3 WRC	

Podium Finishes
Monte Carlo: Atkinson 3rd
Mexico: Atkinson 2nd
Jordan: Atkinson 3rd
Acropolis: Solberg 2nd
Finland: Atkinson 3rd

Overall Results
Subaru 3rd in WRC Manufacturers' Championship
Atkinson 5th in WRC Drivers' Championship
Solberg 6th in WRC Drivers' Championship

Subaru embarked on the 2008 WRC season using updated versions of the 2007 cars for the season's first three rallies alongside the new 2008 WRC car. The team was fully composed of new cars from the Rally Argentina in March. For 2008, the SWRT drivers were Petter Solberg (with co-driver Phil Mills) and Chris Atkinson (with

The Finland Rally was the second event in the 2008 season, and Petter Solberg claimed a fourth place with the new hatchback WRC car.

Solberg's car kicks up dust on the second day of the BP Ultimate Rally of Greece, the event formerly known as the Acropolis.

Stéphane Prévot). Brice Tirabassi (with Fabrice Gordon as co-driver) joined for the Catalunya and Corsican events in October.

For this rally season, however, all eyes were on the new 2008 WRC cars. They proved immediately that they were competitive, with Solberg and Atkinson lying second and third respectively on the final day of the Argentina event. Unfortunately, an electrical failure put Solberg's car out of action, but Atkinson drove steadily, took over Solberg's place in the rankings and finished a very creditable second. For their first time out, this was an extremely encouraging result for the new hatchback WRC Imprezas.

But it turned out to be a season of mixed results, with Solberg finishing several times just outside the top three places but frustratingly claiming only one podium place – a second place in the Rally of Greece in June with the 2008 car. Atkinson did rather better, with five podium finishes in the 15 rallies. He achieved second places in Mexico (with a 2007 car) and Argentina, and third in Monte Carlo (again with a 2007 car), the new Jordan event, and Finland. Once again, Subaru finished the season with third place in the Manufacturers' Championship

Even so, it was a creditable series of results in a season dominated by the Ford Focus RS and the Citroën C4 WRC cars, and as a result Subaru's announcement on 16 December that it would not be entering the 2009 WRC series came as a major shock to rally enthusiasts.

Behind the Wheel: The Subaru WRC Drivers, 2008

Chris ATKINSON
Australian Chris Atkinson had been driving for Subaru since 2005. There are more details of his career in Chapter 7.

Petter SOLBERG
Petter Solberg joined the Subaru WRC team in 2000 and became its key driver. There are more details of his career in Chapter 4.

Brice TIRABASSI
Brice Tirabassi drove just twice for the Subaru Wold Rally Team, and was the only new name among the drivers of

the third-generation car for 2008. He had been the French 1600cc champion, won the French Rally Championship in 2002, and entered world rallying through the Junior World Rally Championship in 2003. He took the individual title that year after winning three of the seven rounds. In 2005, he drove in the Production World Rally Championship, and the following year piloted a Citroën in the Junior World Rally Championship, racking up a victory in Corsica. He drove a Peugeot 207 on Intercontinental Rally Challenge events at the start of 2008, and was invited to join Subaru for the two tarmac rounds of the WRC in Catalunya and Corsica.

CHAPTER 11

SPECIAL EDITIONS OF THE THIRD-GENERATION CARS, FROM 2008

There was much less emphasis on special editions of the third-generation turbocharged Impreza, and to a large extent this was because there was no rallying programme and, therefore, no rally successes to use as the focus for promotional activity.

UK SPECIAL EDITIONS

WRX-S (2008)

Unknown Total

The WRX-S was announced at the British International Motor Show on 23 July 2008, although no limit was set on production at the time. The car was based on the hatchback body and incorporated a number of items from the STI catalogue. The list price was £22,495.

Bodywork:
Available in Obsidian Black Pearl, San Remo Red, Satin White Pearl or WR Blue Mica.
STI front grille.
STI front lip spoiler.
STI rear wing and body-colour tailgate moulding.
Rear diffuser.

Interior:
Leather-trimmed steering wheel.
ICE system with radio and six-disc CD player; 10 speakers.
Momo Air-Race gear knob.

Engine:
2457cc engine with 255PS (252bhp) at 5400rpm and 390Nm (288lb ft) at 3000rpm.
Modified exhaust system.

Running gear:
Anthracite-finish GT1 7.5Jx18-inch five-spoke alloy wheels with 225/40 tyres.

WRX STI 330S (2008)

Unknown Total

The STI 330S was announced at the British International Motor Show on 23 July 2008, although no example of the car was actually on display and deliveries did not begin until September. At the time, Subaru UK did not state how many examples were to be built. The 330S was based on the hatchback body and the modifications were by Prodrive. The car cost £30,000.

Bodywork:
Available in Obsidian Black Pearl, San Remo Red, Satin White Pearl or WR Blue Mica.
STI front grille.
STI front lip spoiler.
Xenon headlamps.
STI rear wing and body-colour tailgate moulding.
Rear diffuser.
330S badge on tailgate.

Interior:
Leather-trimmed steering wheel.

The WRX-S was available only as a hatchback, but added more performance to the standard WRX model.

THIS PAGE AND OVERLEAF: *The WRX STI 330S was an attractive upgrade of the basic WRX STI hatchback model, developed with assistance from long-term partners, Prodrive.*

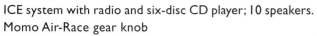

ICE system with radio and six-disc CD player; 10 speakers. Momo Air-Race gear knob

Keyless 'Smart Entry' system and ignition, with push-button start.

Engine:
2457cc engine with 330PS (325bhp) at 5400rpm and 447Nm (347lb ft) at 3400rpm.

Special exhaust system with 90mm (3.6in) stainless-steel pipes.

Suspension:
Anthracite-finish GT1 8.5Jx18-inch five-spoke alloy wheels with 225/40 tyres.

Cosworth Impreza STI CS400 (2010)

75 Examples

The Cosworth Impreza was a UK-only limited edition, based on the hatchback STI model and developed in tandem with UK tuning consultancy Cosworth. It was announced in late May 2010 and cost £49,995.

Bodywork:
Mesh upper grille with piano black finish frame.
Special front bumper.
Cosworth logo on lower mesh grille.
Lip spoiler.
Rear spoiler at top of hatch.

Interior:
Recaro leather seats with Cosworth logo.
Centre console panel in piano black.
Floor mats with Cosworth logo.

Engine:
2457cc engine with 400PS (395bhp).
Cosworth racing pistons with forged connecting rods.
Heavy-duty cylinder-head studs.
Multi-layer head gasket.
High-pressure oil pump.
Remapped ECU.
Turbocharger with redesigned compressor and wastegate actuator.
Larger-capacity tubular exhaust manifold with larger-diameter downpipes.

Running gear:
Uprated clutch.
Front ride height lowered by 15mm (0.6in).
Bilstein struts.
Eibach springs.
Larger AP Racing ventilated front discs with six-piston calipers.
18-inch Pro-Race alloy wheels in Anthracite Grey.

THIS PAGE AND OVERLEAF: *The STI CS400 was a very special development by renowned tuning specialists Cosworth for the UK market only. It was formidably expensive but succeeded in drawing much-needed attention to the high-performance Impreza range.*

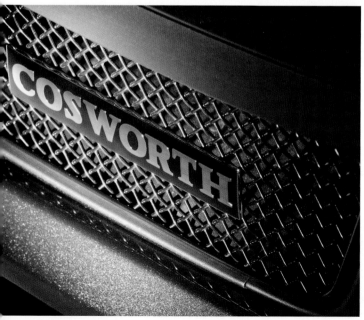

JAPANESE SPECIAL EDITIONS

20th Anniversary Edition WRX STI (2009)

300 Examples

The 20th Anniversary Edition was announced in October 2008 to celebrate 20 years of Subaru's STI high-performance division, and became available in January 2009. It was based on the WRX STI hatchback model and cost 4,126,500 yen in Japan.

Bodywork:
All cars finished in white.
Front lip spoiler.
Blacked-out rear spoiler.
Special badges.
Body kit.

Interior:
Recaro seats.
Leather-trimmed gear knob.

Engine:
1994cc engine with 300PS (304bhp).

Running gear:
Stiffer front wishbones.
New anti-roll bars.
Re-tuned dampers and springs.
Revised suspension mounts and bushes.

18-inch 12-spoke cast alloy wheels.

WRX STI Spec C (2009)

900 Examples
The Spec C car was released in Japan on 23 July 2009. The 'C' stood for 'Competition', and the model was based on the hatchback body. It featured an aluminium bonnet and lightweight glass to save weight.

Bodywork:
Available in Pure White or Sunrise Yellow (but press pictures also showed a blue car).
Aluminium bonnet.
Lightweight laminar window glass.

Interior:
Recaro front sports seats.
Optional alcantara and leather upholstery.
Puncture repair kit instead of space-saver spare wheel.

Engine:
1994cc engine with 304PS (300bhp) and 430Nm (317lb ft).
Turbocharger with reduced-friction axle bearings.
Remapped ECU.
Intercooler water spray.
Lightweight battery.

Running gear:
Lowered ride height.
Stiffer springs.

For the 20th anniversary of Subaru Tecnica International, Japan received a special WRX STI model.

Part of the essence of every Japanese special edition were unique cosmetic items; these two were found on the 2010 R205 model.

Larger-diameter front and rear anti-roll bars.
Front strut brace.
Rear LSD.
Gold-painted Brembo brake calipers.
Lightweight 18-inch alloy wheels with seven split spokes.
Bridgestone Potenza 245-section tyres.
Optional 17-inch alloy wheels.

R205 (2010)

400 Examples

The R205 edition was announced in Japan on 7 January 2010. The 'R' in the name stood for 'Road Sport'. The model was based on the hatchback WRX STI and cost 4,510,000 Yen. STI claimed that some of the parts new for the R205 had been tested on a WRX STI that ran in the 2009 Nürburgring 24-hour race.

Bodywork:
Unique black grille.
Special front spoiler.
Special side skirts.
STI front wing trims in black.
Black rear roof spoiler.
New rear diffuser.
R205 badges on grille and tailgate.

Interior:
Side sill plates with R205 logos.
Limited edition number-plate.
Optional SI-Drive.

Engine:
1994cc engine with 320PS (325bhp) and 431Nm (317lb ft).
Turbocharger with ball-bearing turbine axle.
Remapped ECU.
Exhaust with lower back pressure and sports silencer.

Running gear:
STI springs and dampers; inverted front struts.
Flexible front strut brace.
Flexible brace on lower front suspension arms.
Uprated front anti-roll bar.
Brembo brakes with grooved discs; six-piston front calipers and four-piston rears. Silver logo on calipers.
18-inch 12-spoke cast alloy wheels.
Bridgestone Potenza RE70 245/40R18 tyres.

S206 (2012)

300 Examples
The S206 was announced on 24 November 2011 as a limited edition exclusive to the Japanese market. All cars were four-door saloons based on the WRX STI. Of the 300 built, 100 were special NBR Challenge Package models, celebrating Subaru's SP3T class win at the June 2011 24-hour Nürburgring race.

Bodywork:
Special front spoiler.
Special rear spoiler.
Carbon-fibre roof and carbon-fibre rear spoiler on NBR Challenge Package models.

Interior:
Recaro racing seats.
Leather-trimmed steering wheel.

Engine:
1994cc engine with 316bhp and 318lb ft torque.
New twin-scroll turbocharger.
Upgraded ECU.
Sports exhaust.
Larger intercooler.

Redesigned air filter.

Running gear:
Bilstein struts, coils and dampers.
Front strut brace.
Brembo brakes.

AUSTRALIAN SPECIAL EDITIONS

WRX Club Spec 10 (2010)

250 Examples
The 2010 Club Spec limited edition was announced in May that year. It was based on the four-door saloon model and cost $49,990.

Bodywork:
Available in Obsidian Black, Satin White and WR Blue.
STI front lip spoiler.
Sunroof.
CS10 special edition badges.

Interior:
Leather upholstery.
Satellite navigation system.

Engine:
2457cc WRX engine.

Running gear:
Flexible front strut brace.
Flexible lower front suspension support kit.
8J x 17 lightweight 12-spoke Enkei alloy wheels.

IDENTIFICATION

An Impreza's 17-digit Vehicle Identification Number (VIN) conforms to internationally agreed standards and can be found on a plate attached to the inner wing on the right-hand side (looking forwards) of the engine bay. It is also on the bulkhead. From 2003 onwards, it is also found on a plastic plate fixed to the dash on the left-hand side of the car and visible through the windscreen. There are two different VIN systems in use, one generally used in Japan, Europe and certain other territories, and the other used in the USA and some other territories.

JAPANESE AND EUROPEAN VINS

The VIN code consists of a alphanumeric string of 17 digits and letters. The first 11 elements identify the build specification of the car. As a theoretical example, JF1GC8A48D543210 would break down as follows (with alternatives):

J   Japan (country of origin)
F   Fuji Heavy Industries
I   Passenger car
G   Impreza
C   Saloon (1993–2000; GC series)
     D = Saloon (2001–2007; GD series)
     E = Saloon (2008 on; GE series)
     F = Sports Wagon (1993–2000)
     G = Sports Wagon (2001–2007)
     H = Hatchback (2008 on)
     M = Two-door (1993–2000)
     R = Wide-body hatchback (2008 on)
8   1994cc turbocharged engine
     4 = 2212cc turbocharged engine

     6 = 2457cc turbocharged engine
     7 = 2457cc turbocharged STI engine (2001–2007)
     7 = 2457cc turbocharged engine (2008 on)
     8 = 2457cc turbocharged STI engine (2008 on)
A   1993 model-year
     B = 1994 model-year
     C = 1995 and 1996 model-years
     D = 1997 model-year
     E = 1998 model-year
     F = 1999 model-year
     G = 2000 model-year
     1 = 2001 model-year
     2 = 2002 model-year
     3 = 2003 model-year
     4 = 2004 model-year
     5 = 2005 model-year
     6 = 2006 model-year
     7 = 2007 model-year
     8 = 2008 model-year
     9 = 2009 model-year
     0 = 2010 model-year
     1 = 2011 model-year
     2 = 2012 model-year
4   Four-door body (saloon)
     2 = Two-door body (coupé)
     5 = Five-door body (Sports Wagon, 1993–2007)
     5 = Five-door body (Hatchback, 2008 on)
8   WRX model (1993–2000)
     7 = RA model (1993–2000)
     9 = WRX model (2001 on)
     0 = WRX STI model (2001 on)
     D = STI Type R and RA (1993–2000)
     E = STI model (from Version III, 1997 model-year, to 2000)

S = 22B model

D   Four-speed manual gearbox (1993–2000)

          G = Five-speed manual gearbox (2001 on)

          H = Four-speed automatic (2001 on)

          L = Six-speed manual (2001 on)

          P = Four-speed automatic (1993-2000)

543210 Serial number

400001 series for two-door coupés (1995–2000)

500001 series for four-door saloons

800001 series for five-door Sports Wagons

US-STYLE VINS

The VIN code consists of a alphanumeric string of 17 digits and letters. The first 11 elements identify the build specification of the car. For example, JF1GD255XNG567890 would break down as follows (with alternatives):

J   Japan (country of origin)

F   Fuji Heavy Industries

I   Passenger car

G   Impreza

D   Saloon (second-generation or GD series)

          E = Saloon (third-generation or GE series)

          G = Sports Wagon (2001-2007)

          H = Hatchback (2008 on)

          R = Hatchback with wide body

2   1994cc turbocharged engine

          7 = 2.5-litre turbocharged engine

          8 = 2.5-litre turbocharged STI engine

9   WRX model

          0 = WRX STI model

5   Manual seat belts with dual front airbags

          6 = Manual seat belts with dual front and dual side airbags

X   Check digit (may also be 0–9)

N   1992 model-year

          P = 1993 model-year

          R = 1994 model-year

          S = 1995 model-year

          T = 1996 model-year

          V = 1997 model-year

          W =1998 model-year

          X = 1999 model-year

          Y = 2000 model-year

          1 = 2001 model-year

          2 = 2002 model-year

          3 = 2003 model-year

          4 = 2004 model-year

          5 = 2005 model-year

          6 = 2006 model-year

          7 = 2007 model-year

          8 = 2008 model-year

          9 = 2009 model-year

          0 = 2010 model-year

          1 = 2011 model-year

          2 = 2012 model-year

G   All-wheel drive, five-speed manual gearbox

          H = All-wheel drive, automatic gearbox

          L = All-wheel drive, six-speed manual gearbox

567890 Serial number

500001 series for four-door saloons

600001 series for five-door hatchbacks (2008 on)

800001 series for Sports Wagons (2001–2007)

INDEX